"Straightforward clear advic
with your Older Man. Vranich and Grashow break it down
into usable, cutting-edge information that forces you to
think and figure out the hard issues around love."

— Dr. Ian Kerner,
author of *She Comes First*,
and *He Comes Next*

ॐ

"Whether he's five years older or fifteen, this book is essential
in navigating the different issues dating an older man brings
up. It's a whole different ballgame and clear good advice like
this is priceless."

— Ariane Marder,
Men's Fitness Sex Editor

ॐ

"*Dating the Older Man* is two books for the price of one. The
first deals with the ups and downs of a romantic relationship
the authors delicately label as an OM (older man). The second offers a guide to navigating the network of connections
that are part of life with an OM. For women, challenges can
come from friends who question their mental status, potential stepchildren who regard them as rivals for their father's
attention, and female family members who arch their eyebrows in unspoken judgment. The authors provide plenty
of guidance on how to deal with both the OM and the cast
of characters around him through case studies, quotes from
their clinical practice, and advice grounded in sound thera-
peutic principles."

— Cheryl Dellasega, Ph.D.,
author of *Surviving Ophelia*,
Mean Girls Grown Up, and *Girl Wars*

dating
O*the*lder
MAN

Consider Your Differences and Decide If He's Right for You

Belisa Vranich, Psy.D. and
Laura Grashow, Psy.D.

Avon, Massachusetts

Published by
Adams Media, an F+W Publications Company
57 Littlefield Street, Avon, MA 02322. U.S.A.
www.adamsmedia.com

ISBN-10: 1-59869-818-4
ISBN-13: 978-1-59869-818-3

Printed in the United States of America.

J I H G F E D C B A

Library of Congress Cataloging-in-Publication Data
is available from the publisher.

This publication is designed to provide accurate and authoritative information with regard to the subject matter covered. It is sold with the understanding that the publisher is not engaged in rendering legal, accounting,
or other professional advice. If legal advice or other expert assistance is
required, the services of a competent professional person should be sought.
—From a *Declaration of Principles* jointly adopted by a
Committee of the American Bar Association and a
Committee of Publishers and Associations

Many of the designations used by manufacturers and sellers to distinguish
their product are claimed as trademarks. Where those designations appear
in this book and Adams Media was aware of a trademark claim, the designations have been printed with initial capital letters.

This book is available at quantity discounts for bulk purchases.
For information, please call 1-800-289-0963.

Contents

introduction

Love in the Time of Agelessness

The stereotype of the man caught in a midlife crisis is a well-known one: He gets himself a sports car and has an affair with the much younger secretary. You also know the couple that flaunts each other: One saying, "He can afford me," and the other saying, "I can afford her." The caricature that was Anna Nicole Smith and J. Howard Marshall—this book is *not* about them.

This book is about the revised older-man/younger-woman duo, a scenario in which, given rejuvenation and the push for eternal youth and extension of life, the "younger" woman may be thirty-five or forty, and the older man ten to twenty years older. He may not necessarily be rich or have "bought" her. His *joie de vivre*, his appreciation of her, and the mature take on life he possesses—one that younger men lack—have made her consider him a candidate. They may not even look odd together. Age, then, has really become just a number.

This book is for women who decide to take a chance on an older man, accepting the notion that love is ageless. They themselves may be in their twenties, thirties, or for-ties—not the stereotypical hot young bimbo that comes to mind. These women have come into our offices with questions never raised before . . . seeking real information and examining issues related to the fact that they were raised in different generations than their significant other. This is the woman who has decided that she is going to broaden her playing field. Men have always had the choice to marry up, down, or sideways; no one really objected or criticized. Unfortunately for women, there has existed a narrower definition of what is appropriate—until today.

There have been numerous changes in our society. Life expectancy has crept upward and upward; Internet dating is bringing people together who never would have met otherwise; advances in medicine that have us all more spry— regardless of age—than our parents or grandparents; and, most important, the mindset has evolved that chronological age and "real age" are different things. We live in a culture of aging well.

In Her Words

"I remember telling myself he's too old for me rather than telling myself that I am too young for him. Then I thought, why? It was like I was having an argument with myself. I remember cautiously asking a friend if she thought he was attractive."

Kelly, 39

While neither of us are sociologists or cultural anthropologists—so we can't critique this cultural trend—we have written this book as an informed response to having more nontraditional couples seek therapy, especially women who are choosing to date older men when they never would have done so before.

Some women started dating older men deliberately, wanting a bigger dating pool. Others were caught by surprise as they found a coworker attractive—one whom they never would have considered desirable before. All were struggling with the ways in which they would be perceived, the stark and subtle differences between dating peers or younger men and older guys, and issues related to the dynamics between them.

Being a couple is hard enough. Can dating a man older than you make some of this easier?

one

Are You Ready for an Older Man?

Turn on any daytime soap or chick flick and you'll see that love conquers a lot—even a generation gap. But if you're the younger woman for the first time in your life, it can be a little scary, especially if few of your girlfriends can relate and commiserate. While there are tons of books and Web sites that aim to teach the newly single older man how to nab a younger women, where are the resources for you? Well, here you have it: a how-to manual on creating a successful relationship with an older man, a discussion of your thoughts and struggles—a roadmap for "the younger woman." This book is for you.

Our aim is to help you fit your new relationship into your current life, teach you effective ways to silence your critics, and keep those you love close. You'll learn what to expect (emotionally, intellectually, and physically) from an older man, as well as effective ways to develop authentic relationships with his family.

Dating men the same age as you or younger can simply be too much work. Chances are you're more likely to deal with commitment jitters, career meltdowns, priority muddles, and roommates instead of romance, dinner, and fun. Amy, thirty-one, puts it succinctly: "A guy under thirty tends to be a workaholic who has fit you into his schedule only to remain conflicted about what he wants. He's looking at what his friends have; he's worried that he'll miss something if he's exclusive with you, and he's not sure if he's supposed to be sensitive or manly, or how to be both successfully. Too much trouble."

In Her Words
"One time my friend Jodie's uncle came to visit her. He was ten years younger than her dad, twelve years older than me. I remember thinking he was kind of cute, in that 'older guy kind of way.' When he smiled at me and didn't look away I was caught off guard. Did he find me pretty instead of cute? Did I misread his cues?"

Elise, 22

Some wonder if the state of men younger than thirty has something to do with so many being the product of divorce. One hypothesis is that a large number of boys born in the late 1970s were raised without fathers, which means our population may be filled with a generation of guys who never learned how to be "real" men. Whatever the reason, more and more women are finding younger men and men close to their age less and less appealing—and society's standards are catching up. Pursuing a relationship with a more mature, established older man—even ten, fifteen years your senior— is becoming progressively more acceptable in today's world. The top two cited reasons? "He looks good" and he "knows how to treat a woman." Modern men are aging gracefully, or not aging at all. Our culture now perceives birth date or chronological age as something very different than "real age" or "body age."

Statistics tell us the older-man/younger-woman couple will continue to become more and more prevalent—in part, because men are living longer than ever before and looking and acting more youthful than ever before, whereas women are waiting longer to marry, and because divorces from first (and second) marriages continue to rise. What this means is that more women in their late twenties, thirties, and forties are widening their "date span" to include men significantly older than themselves.

> ♆ Date span is the age range that you'll consider when dating. What is your date span? Is it very narrow and exclusive? Have you allowed yourself to push the limits so that you have more options?

Why so many women prefer older men and why society is now accepting this phenomenon may be chalked up to perpetuated myths as well as hard science. You've heard it all before—"girls mature faster" or "men are incapable of settling down before forty." Is there any truth to this? There may be. According to studies in the field of medical anthropology, women are predisposed to mating with men who can be good providers, and, according to census and economic literature, men still make more money on average. Add the wisdom that typically comes with life experience and more free time to put into the relationship, and you have a man whom you'd be a fool to discount simply because of his chronological age.

While the younger-woman/older-man relationship is quickly gaining acceptance in our culture, its success ultimately depends on the individual couple. If all of the sudden you find yourself in a relationship that may raise eyebrows or prompt chuckles, it can be stressful. For some, being on the end of inquiring stares (whether imaginary or real) is too much to bear. To make things worse, limited resources when it comes to commiseration and venting may feel like a real lack of support. But, hey, we wrote this book because we believe, after polling and interviewing hundreds of couples, that a relationship with an older man can be a great experience.

In Her Words

"All I heard about growing up were divorces and infidelities. So you know what, I am just going to go out with the guy that makes me happy and appreciates me more. All these rules of who is right and how we should do things, for what?"

Kimberly, 29

Older? Yes. Wiser? Maybe

Dating an older man may catapult you right over some of the more typical initial relationship hurdles, but it could also land you in the face of challenges you never anticipated. Sure, he's confident, experienced, financially secure, and loves having you at his side, but dating an older man isn't necessarily easier than being with someone your age. Instead of reaming out your boyfriend over a weekend bender with his pledge class, you're dealing with his ex-wife (who may feel abandoned and neglected), his children (who may not instantly love you), his friends and their wives (who may very well judge you before they've even met you), and your parents (who may be judging him in the same way).

If it all sounds daunting, remember that in spite of this bevy of complex problems, you can breathe a sigh of relief.

Finally, you're with a man who is more mature than anyone you've ever dated before, has mastered his profession, and seems better equipped to listen and understand what you're saying. While sex, money, personal improvement, material possessions, and status are younger men's primary interests and motivational forces—and their "me" mentality has not yet matured into a "we" philosophy—older men are a whole different smoke, so to speak. They have had more time and experience to learn what physically, emotionally, and intellectually satisfies a woman. In general, women assume very different roles in the lives of their men depending on the age of the men they are dating.

In Her Words
"Divorced doesn't always mean damaged goods. I left my 'starter husband' because I was bored. Our kids were in college and we'd really grown apart and were living more like friends. I'm now engaged to a man who is far better suited for me at this time in my life. I hope my ex does the same; he's a great guy, he deserves it."

Lynn, 40

Maybe your initial attraction to an older man took you by surprise. Perhaps you'd never considered other men his age, but somehow he slipped between the cracks of your age "requirements." It wasn't that you eased into dating men ten years older by first dating men two, three, five, and six years your senior. On the contrary—it was "Bam!"—right in the middle of a sentence he smiled, and it hit you right in the solar plexus. You were stunned, and maybe even aghast, to catch yourself flirting with him. At the very least, you were probably perplexed.

Was there a specific catalyst for this attraction? Did you gradually get "fed up" with dating guys closer to your age? Did you make a concerted effort to widen the age range of potential mates, sick of being criticized by your mother for still being single because you're "too picky"? Maybe you realized that your narrow definition of Prince Charming wasn't realistic, plus your friends who actually did ride off into the sunset with guys close to their age are now getting separated, divorced, and/or having affairs. Or maybe it was sudden and unexpected, and you have no idea how to explain it.

> ♫ The number one reason women interviewed for this book like their older fella: "He picks his battles and lets a lot slide." Young bucks, listen up—here are the next most popular reasons:
> *"He really makes it a point to have fun."*
> *"He's less of a workaholic."*
> *"All his actions don't need to be translated—he doesn't play games."*
> *"He likes his job, and is confident about what he does."*

Whatever the origins of your attraction, this book is designed to help you get the most out of a relationship with an older man; to make wise choices for the relationship and for yourself; to follow your heart yet not lose your head; and to build something that brings you fulfillment.

The Awe Factor: Why He's Looking at You

Maureen Dowd, journalist and author of *Are Men Necessary?* theorized to *The Washington Post* that "successful men don't want fascinating women, they just want women who are awed by them." Men who date younger women often find that the amount of awe bestowed upon them is more than they ever got from a contemporary significant other. Of course this is not always the case. It depends on how many independent interests you pursue and how established your career is, as well as how accomplished your professional circle is. The bottom line is that even though you may be fiercely career-driven and business-savvy, you probably not only give your older man appreciation where it's due, but also continue to be wowed by his experience and confidence, and get especially charged up by it.

According to classic psychological theory, he's probably at a stage where recognition for his accomplishments is more important to his psychological well-being than it was when he was younger and than it will be when he's older. A number of men interviewed for this book stated that it was the younger woman's emotional availability that was so attractive—how much attention they gave, the openness to experience anything, and how important they made their men feel.

To you, he's capable, experienced, wise, representative of stability and security, and may even be a great candidate for fatherhood. Your older boyfriend may strike you as the height of intellect and maturity—especially when he's dependable, faithful, and can lend an understanding shoulder to cry on when you've had a crappy day at work.

And what exactly do you represent to him? Does your boyfriend exclusively date younger women? Have you heard him utter words such as "Women over forty really don't do much for me"? Or, is he more open to a wider range of ages, yet has fallen in love with you spontaneously because of chemistry? Whatever the case, the choice by men to pursue younger women is attributed to a host of psychological and biological needs. This relationship makeup has roots in history and can be explained scientifically.

On a very basic, biological level, vitality is one of the things men are wired to seek in a mate. In ancient times, women in Mesopotamia stained their cheeks with wild berry juice to appear more flushed, and thus more vital. The women who looked as if they could have the most babies and survive childbirth propagated the human species. That's why, in modern times, being with a younger woman can actually propel an older guy into a "propagating" state of mind—even if when you met him he felt as if he had enough offspring from a prior marriage. Feeling as if he "still has it" goes a long way when looking for a new lease on life, especially if he's at an age where he's realizing that someday he's going to kick the bucket and wants to feel alive now!

People are not just about primal instincts, and love is more complex than just the propagation of the species. The great thing about the attraction to youth is that you don't have to be such a youngster in order to offer yourself up as a vital woman who also still has a lot of life in her. Even if your age difference is small, it is your vitality that acts as a potent elixir for his desire to be around you. Numerous men interviewed for this book said that, after physical attraction, it is vitality, openness to life, and self-confidence that they find most attractive in women. Moreover, they stated that when the initial physical attraction wanes, it is these qualities that stoke the fire of love—not breast implants or Botox. As one man so aptly told us, "You [can] get older but you don't [have to] age" if you "continuously use your brain in creative ways and keep your body healthy."

It's one thing to seek out vitality and excitement in a mate and quite another to surround yourself with pretty accoutrements in an attempt to look better and hold onto some youth. If you can't shake a nagging feeling that you (along with his Mercedes convertible) are playing equal roles in his midlife crisis, do stay on guard. We're not saying there aren't older men out there who take on young women like an expensive purchase and parade them around town like a fancy show piece. We're just saying that there's a well-documented biological basis for the likelihood of older men to genuinely fall in love with younger women.

INDICATORS THAT YOU'RE A PART OF A MIDLIFE CRISIS:

- He introduces you to his friends and they nod and wink.
- He refers to himself as your "sugar daddy."
- He no longer acts like his normal fifty-something self but insists on attending college parties, beer pong tournaments, and hanging out at the bars around the corner from your university.
- He uses hip twenty-something lingo (and sounds incredibly awkward while doing so).

Older Stereotypes, Younger Stereotypes

Not all older men are wiser, more financially stable, sensitive, or secure. One stereotype of the older man depicts him as doting, suave, and grateful for the renewed lease on life that the younger girlfriend has given him. Other cartoonish versions have him turning in hours before his younger spouse, being sexually sedate, and making references to classic movies set in the 1950s or music and pop culture that she's only familiar with from seeing *Back to the Future*.

The younger girlfriend or younger second wife continues to take a beating in the stereotype department as well: She's a gold digger, a home wrecker, and nothing more than the object of a midlife crisis. She may be accused of going after his professional knowledge and contacts, his insurance, money, and credit, and of creating strife between him and his adult children. The media is saturated with relationships like Anna Nicole Smith's (twenty-six) with J. Howard Marshall (eighty-nine), or Hugh Hefner's (eighty-two) with his three bunnies (thirty, thirty-five, and twenty-three), which have only added fuel to the fire.

In Her Words
Projected anxiety is the amount of time you spend worrying how long you'll get along before he is too old for you. "Let's say I'm twenty-six and dating someone who is forty. Still hot, still sexy, still great in bed. Then I turn forty and he's almost fifty-five. I'm still going out with my girlfriends, still healthy, still working out every day; he, on the other hand, might not be able to keep up and might impact my social life since I have to stay at home and rub arthritis cream on his joints."

Krissy, 28

Women generally gravitate toward (at least slightly) older men. The marriage announcements in the *New York Times*, though peppered with second marriages and same-sex marriages, feature mostly heterosexual couples in which the guy is about two years older. The public is practically bored to tears by tabloid headlines such as those announcing Michael Douglas's marriage to Catherine Zeta Jones—she's twenty-five years his junior. Likewise, the wedding between fifty-four-year-old Billy Joel and twenty-three-year-old Katie Lee failed to produce any public controversy, and neither did the marriage of Kate Hudson, twenty-seven, to the Black Crowes Chris Robinson, thirty-nine. The age difference between Nick Lachey, twenty-nine, and Jessica Simpson, twenty-two, or Paul McCartney, fifty-nine, and

Heather Mills, thirty-three, was never publicly factored into the deterioration of their marriages. Even favorite fictional heroines date significantly older men. Carrie Bradshaw, of *Sex and the City*, was in her thirties and routinely dated older men (and wound up in the long haul with Mr. Big, the well-to-do bachelor in his forties).

🐦 You know the older-man/younger-woman relationship is socially acceptable (and the reverse is unfortunately not) when, at fifty-four, Billy Joel married a twenty-three-year-old Katie Lee to absolutely no public controversy, whereas, at the same time, the media had a full-out frenzy when Demi Moore wed her beau Ashton Kutcher, who is sixteen years her junior.

When exactly does the age difference between two sweethearts start to raise eyebrows? If you're not a celebrity, it's about seven years (though the number starts out much smaller and then plateaus later in life) or when the new stepmother and stepdaughters in the family photo look closer in age than anyone else. If it's you in the hot seat, you start to get an idea of how open- or closed-minded the people are around you when the probing questions about your respective college graduation dates start flying.

We polled women in relationships with significantly older men, and here's what they were the most anxious about:

"People would mistake us for father and daughter."—Lisa, 26 (Mark, 45)

"The assumption that I was after something—a promotion or access to his wallet."—Karen, 36 (Keith, 48)

"Not being taken seriously, like I was the answer to his midlife crisis or something."—Felicia, 30 (Chris, 44)

"Those thinking, 'Whew, she has unresolved father issues since this guy is obviously more like a dad to her than a boyfriend.'"—Jenny, 31 (Tom, 46)

"Not being able to fill his first wife's shoes—'Sheila did it like this, Sheila never did that . . . '—I felt like we'd never be two people dating, always three."—Caren, 35 (Paul, 54)

Kicking and Screaming into Old Age

Chronological age has little to do with how you act, look, and feel. In fact, according to Suzanne Braun Levine, author of *Inventing the Rest of Our Lives: Women in Second Adulthood*, women can all look forward to two adulthoods: "If you figure that the first adulthood lasts from twenty-five to fifty, you have statistically at least that much time ahead of you until you're seventy-five."

While your chemistry together is largely connected to physical appearance, it's far from everything. A man who knows and likes himself well enough to not be competitive or pejorative, and is secure enough to admit his mistakes and laugh at himself, can seem handsome even if he's not conventionally good looking—and that kind of handsome outlasts any spare tires or gray hairs that might come his way.

A Strange Trip— When Two Realities Don't Become One

As a little girl you might have daydreamed about your wedding, or as a young adult thought about growing old with your husband and going through life's trials and tribulations together at the same pace. Together, you'd deal with developing and maintaining careers, raising kids from infancy through college, caring for your aging parents, and counting on your adult children to care for you when the time came. When you're with an older man, this daydream will be nothing like reality.

Chronology disparity is the term used when a difference in age means that each person in a couple experiences age-related events years apart from each other. In other words, when spouses are close in age life changes happen in unison, whereas for a couple in which one of the people is significantly older, age-related events happen at significantly different times and result in significantly different experiences.

In Her Words

"Most of the guys I'd gone out with were my age or two to three years older. Max had almost a whole decade. At first I figured he was slightly older; when I found out his age, all of the sudden I started looking for things that made us different. I was sure there had to be too many. I was sure people could see our age difference when we walked around. Sometimes I felt like that is what they were thinking and snickering behind our backs. In retrospect that was silly. We look like a couple. He's forty-two."

Louisa, 33

Though this may not be a familiar scenario, it's not necessarily a bad one. When stressful chronology events, such as caring for parents, retirement, career peaks, and various phases of sexuality happen in unison, partners close in age may be unable to provide enough emotional support to each other. Older-man/younger-woman relationships mean his parents age at least a decade before hers. As both partners experience caring for the aged, she can be better prepared, both practically and psychologically, for when her time comes to care for her husband and parents (perhaps simultaneously).

May-December Romance

This classic term is applied to a relationship where there is an age discrepancy, but maybe this label sounds way too demure for what you are experiencing.

This phenomenon of staggered chronology seems to have the power to systematically destroy the notion of the wide-eyed younger woman and her stereotypically more submissive role. After all, we're talking about the new "modern younger woman" who may in fact be in her thirties or forties, and who has come of age in an era when women are waiting longer to get married because they are enjoying their careers and independence. Forget demure, honey; you haven't known *submissive* in the classic sense. You've hit the ground running, and the combination of your youth, energy, strength, lessons learned from career pursuits, and experience from going through life-cycle stressors with him illustrates how the disparity in age can actually redistribute power with more equality and can make getting things done more efficient. More important, from a relationship standpoint, what you have here sounds more like psychologically equal partners who must collaborate to survive—and this is what many women crave.

Voila! There you have it: efficiency and mental health. This notion really does turn Little Miss Demure and Submissive into nothing more than a character in a fairytale. In fact, it could also keep you from splitting up. Today's high rates of divorce and infidelity suggest that dual chronology may play an important role in putting undue strain on a relationship and may be, at least partly, to blame for the breakup. Ah, behold the advantages of chronology disparity.

> ♪♪ Don't trade in your stilettos for Naturalizers. The worst thing a woman can do is to assume she has to look more mature (trying to catch up to him to make their age difference seem less obvious). Maybe the reason he was initially attracted to you is your irreverent streak—for instance, your ability to pull off a good pair of Chuck Taylors. Do revel in the fact that no matter how old you are, you will *always* be the younger woman to him.

Can't Buy Me Love

Statistics tell us he'll probably be more financially stable than your younger ex-boyfriends (and he'll probably have a better perspective on money and happiness, too). Unlike the stereotype of the older man owning and paying for his younger arm candy, you appreciate his financial stability in that it can make for less worry and be helpful in allowing you to pursue your career goals more freely.

> ♪♪ Experian, one of the three premier credit-reporting agencies, notes that the average female in the age range of forty-five through fifty-nine carries $11,414 in revolving debt. And, according to the AARP Foundation's women's study, divorced women and women ages forty-five through forty-nine were the least likely to pay off their credit cards each month.

Few women we spoke to described their OM (older man) as a "meal ticket." In fact, most liked the fact that his financial stability made him a calmer person, helped financially with their own careers, and provoked fewer negative feelings, like guilt regarding money. The bottom line is that this group of women is not looking to be a "trophy wife" but does list "the security factor" as one of the attractive parts of the relationship.

> "Elliot being financially stable let me go back to school and finish my degree."—Ginnie, 35

> "George helped me pay for my kids' school. He didn't have to, but it showed how much he cared for me and them."—Felicia, 48

> "I'd pick up weekend shifts just to make ends meet. I didn't really want to quit my job, but working less hours was nice."—Carmela, 29

The Math Game and the "Half-Your-Age-Plus-Seven" Rule

The age difference that is generally accepted by modern society varies directly with the age of the individuals involved in the relationship; that is, larger differences are more acceptable with older individuals. For example, while an eight-year difference might be considered unacceptable (and illegal) between a twenty-three-year-old and a fifteen-year-old, it is less remarkable between a thirty-year-old and a twenty-two-year-old, and generally unnoticed completely between a fifty-eight-year-old and a fifty-year-old. The "half-your-age-plus-seven" rule is a mathematical formula that purports to judge whether the age difference in an intimate relationship is socially acceptable. For instance, a twenty-six-year-old woman could consider a forty-six year old man as a possible mate and still be within the socially acceptable range of the rule.

ᔟ While Hollywood is to blame for perpetuating many negative stereotypes of both younger women and older men, in our focus groups we found that "the graying of Hollywood" also helped a generation of women see that men age gracefully. George Clooney and Richard Gere both come up regularly when women talked about sexy older men. So did Steven Tyler (fifty-nine), John Travolta (fifty-three), Paul Newman (eighty-three), Sylvester Stallone (sixty-one), and Jack Lalane (ninety-two).

"The Math Game," when couples laugh over what each was doing at different ages, can help deflate the anxiety over their ages. "In the beginning of the relationship we'd each do math and keep it to ourselves. Once we got more comfortable, we'd laugh out loud," says Marie, age thirty-two, about her fiancé, age fifty-two. "Some things I still keep to myself; for instance, that he'll collect social security two decades before I do."

In Her Words

"All I knew is I wanted my next boyfriend to be happy with himself and grateful for what he had. I was tired of men who were pessimistic and insecure. I think Bob's having been through a lot gave him perspective. He just complained less and let things go more easily."

Linda, 45

two

Older Man Traits

An older man can be a veritable treasure trove of relation-ship experience: long-term, short-lived, loving, impulsive, complex, or simple. The goal in this chapter is to tell you what certain specific behaviors may imply regarding longevity of a relationship, and to teach you to "crack the code" on the basis of present-day behavior. Since older men have had more life experience, patterns of behavior are easier to see . . . if you know what to look for. Who his exes were and how the relationships started and ended, how he articulates what he wants in the present versus what he wanted in the past—all of this is good information about his expression of love and behavior in a relationship.

Older Man Types: Does This Sound Like Him?

We've categorized a set of personality traits and interpersonal styles, any combination of which you may recognize in a guy with more relationship/life experience. These categories may not cover all men and your man may not fit squarely into any one category, but one (or maybe two) will definitely sound familiar. Most important, they are reflective of what your older man has been through, what he knows intuitively about women and relationships, and what he's learned about them. He might have been married a few years and then divorced, or might have had one girlfriend who turned into his wife, then he was widowed, or he might have been—and still is—the playboy bachelor. . . . Read on to see what you have on your side and what you're up against.

The Wise Guy

No, we aren't being sarcastic here. He is wise. The Wise Guy has patience for the long story. He recognizes and compliments your achievements. He appreciates you for who you are and doesn't try to change you. This is the guy who actually listened during fights and learned new relationship information. (Careful, we aren't saying he learned it when he first had the argument; it may have taken several women with the same argument for him to get it, but now he does!) He gives the impression that he's had sisters and knows how to live with women. Maybe you find yourself wondering when he's going to show his true colors and it's going to end. Don't let past negative experiences lead you to assume that it will all eventually go south. Hang in there.

The Wise Guy has discovered golden nuggets of truth about women, such as:

1. Ignoring an issue won't make it go away; in fact, it usually makes it worse (and don't ever assume she's forgotten).
2. Five minutes of focused attention and the ability to be empathic when she's having a meltdown can save him hours later on.
3. PMS comes every month. Every month she's surprised.

4. "I'm sorry" can mean "I see your point of view" or "I feel for you," not just "you're right." Plus, it gets the fight over with exponentially faster.
5. Doing something that needs to be done without being asked can get him a lot of praise.
6. Being nice to her friends gets him hundreds of points.
7. "I'll make it up to you" sounds great, but the difference is knowing the importance of following through, and actually doing it.
8. Making the effort to sometimes be as polite as when he first met her makes a woman feel happy and appreciated.
9. Remembering what seem to be silly details such as what her drink order is or her favorite author may seem trivial but it makes her feel ecstatic.
10. "Fine," said in the snippy staccato never means "fine." It means trouble.

The Angry Man

He makes a stellar first impression and racks up points on the "positive" side of the scale with ease. Then, either after a few glasses of wine, or once he's comfortable with the relationship, the irritability starts showing through: Compared to a trip to the supermarket with him, reading about Osama Bin Laden seems like a reprieve. And he's pissed at everyone, not just you. His sarcasm runs deep and reflects some really deep-seated anger. He is constantly displacing his anger onto inappropriate targets and personalizing everyone's behaviors even when it's clear to you they have nothing to do with him. Sure, he has good qualities that help you overlook the temper, but his MO is that he is easily irritated by everything and everyone. He has road rage everywhere—at home, in the grocery store, at dinner parties. You never quite know what is going to set him off, or why certain acts or moments make him fly off the handle. Something serious happened in previous relationships and his childhood, but even trying to go down that road when he is unaware and unwilling can make for real trouble. The depth and scope of his anger makes you uncomfortable, and you find yourself trying to be more cheerful than a kids' talk show host, trying to sell trite ideas like "life is too short" and "look at the bright side."

The Wild One

He can't sit still. He comes and goes as he pleases and is up-front about not being good at making plans. "I don't like to be held to anything, I value spontaneity" is the typical mantra. Yes, he's older than you are, but he doesn't always give that impression. He might say that he wants to find love and settle down but his actions say otherwise. He may be acting out after a repressive marriage or had never been married at all (or had the faintest consideration of it). Blasting 1970s rock music in the car and the shower, and getting along with your younger brother as if they are peers may be disturbing, but not calling you for three days at a time, and having the attention span of a garden vegetable can become taxing. On the positive side, you have to admit that this guy can get you to lighten up. At a party, he's the center of attention and friends admire the way he is always in a good mood and ready to go out. And if you're not too frustrated with his flaky ways, the sex can be great. The bottom line here is that sometimes he's a breath of fresh air and sometimes you want to kill him—all within the same ten minutes.

The Victimized and Divorced Guy

"I put all my money into fixing up her place, I put her through school, and I gave her backrubs. . . . She ripped my heart out and stomped on it until every last drop of blood squirted out. I tried harder, brought her flowers, listened, but she wasn't satisfied. But, hey, no biggie, I'm okay. Can you pass the salt?" Confused yet? Translation: "I let her step on me like a doormat and I don't recognize my part in this dynamic. I'm a martyr."

> 🐟 Rick was damn handsome, but, oh, so, bitter. Working together gave Allison the opportunity to hear his life story. He got engaged to his childhood sweetheart and then she pulled a runaway bride and "ruined his life." He fed into Allison's nurturing tendencies but eventually it became clear to her that his victim mentality and tendency to be a doormat oozed into other relationships. His negativity started feeling heavy for her and she began to doubt whether she could shoulder that burden in an ongoing relationship.

This behavior can be described as fishing for reassurance; he's clingy and trying too hard to be loved. Some women relate to feeling so burned, so he can initially come off like a solid, sensitive, dependable guy who would never perpetrate on anyone else what was done to him. Sure, he's available, attentive, and so on, but when is he going to get off the pity pot? And when will it start to get under your skin? Maybe it already has.

The Insecure Guy

Maybe it's chronic or maybe it's a phase. You have to feel your way through this one, and it may take some time to know exactly where he's coming from. Mixed with humor, insecurity can come off as self-deprecation and can even be funny. However, if it's screaming with negativity and self-hatred, it can become quite a drag. The insecure guy needs the awe factor and constant ego stroking to feel good enough about himself to be pleasant company. This is a lot of work, and it doesn't stick. Ultimately, you need to realize that he'll have to get through this by himself or with some sort of therapy. It's possible that his "sensitivity" will become paranoia and his "dependability" smothering.

The Heart-of-Gold Guy

Let's be honest, you never would have talked to this guy ten years ago. He's dorky; he's fodder for *The 40-Year-Old Virgin*. But his sweetness is irresistible, and the confidence that comes with his age and mastery of profession doesn't hurt. Maybe something about him screams, "You can fix me up—all I need is a good haircut, contacts, and for you to choose my clothes," or something of the sort, which makes him a contender. Maybe he brings out the mother in you. Maybe it's the challenge of making him over. The fact is, you are tired of guys with great haircuts and fashionable shoes who are so self-engrossed that they don't even notice when you don't call them back. This guy lights up when he sees you, wags his tail, and takes every opportunity to make you happy . . . then trips on his own shoelaces. (Note to self: Velcro.)

The Control Guy

This protective gentleman slowly crosses the line to controlling and all-consuming. His "take-charge personality" was refreshing at first, but it has become stifling. For him, "trust me" means you ask no questions about anything and I, I, I, will lead the way. While there are moments when you feel you see eye-to-eye and there is equality in the relationship, other times you get flashbacks of an overprotective suspicious dad that you already outgrew, um, a long time ago. He's got other great characteristics but you find yourself taking a deep breath and trying not to scream, "Back off, buddy, I'm not fifteen!" Do you remind him of his adolescence? Was he the oldest sibling? Did his ex-wife encourage this behavior?

It is not impossible to recognize these characteristics and understand where they have come from in order for the relationship to accommodate your perhaps very different personalities and styles. Depending on the discrepancy and how deeply seated his patterns are, it could be damn hard—but, then again, you need to give it a shot, and you can always go back to that scale to look at pros and cons.

> ✍ Lisa, a twenty-seven-year old kindergarten teacher, seethed when her then thirty-nine-year old, divorced boyfriend Tim took her on a corporate trip designed to boost moral on his team, then organized her day and activities from dawn 'til dusk. What initially felt caring was suffocating by the end of the trip. Imagine yourself as a bystander to all this. What unspoken expectations did each of them have? To him, planning his date's day meant he didn't want her to be bored or feel left out, whereas Lisa looked forward to down time where she didn't have to follow a mandatory schedule.

Can He Handle It?

It's safe to say that the most important people in your life are also the ones you want to share your pain with and get support from when you're feeling vulnerable. Safe to say, too, then, that one of those people is your boyfriend. Is he up to it?

Here are some key situations and various responses. It's up to you to decide which situations are most important to you; that is, where you feel you need the most contact and support. There will be responses you love; responses you can live with; and those that, either immediately or over time, become out-and-out deal-breakers. Don't lose sight of the fact that no man and no relationship is perfect, even given the "seasoned veteran" that the older man may be. In the end, the real question is, are you getting enough of what you need to feel happy in the relationship?

One disclaimer for every example of the optimal response is that not every older man is necessarily the wiser man. In many cases, however, experience has played a pivotal role. Many men who have been married or involved in serious, long-term relationships have had the opportunity to learn the effective use of empathy and diplomacy with an emotionally distraught woman. If he is able to listen without criticizing and also give an empathic response, the likelihood is that along the way he has seen the fruits of this response by helping his mate out of a funk, and learned the hard way what makes it worse.

Of course, it's also possible that he got a good start early in life and had a stable relationship with his mother, one in which she was neither too emotionally distant nor too emotionally invasive. In other words, she neither shut him out when she was distraught, nor leaned on him as though he were the husband when she needed support. Instead, she may have been able to talk with him about feelings, label them, help him with self-awareness and self-control, and model productive resolutions with others. Dad also may have played a pivotal role as a man with good skills who interacted with his wife in an effective, compassionate way. As a result, this OM could have learned the basic skills at an early age, which would likely set the stage for further, healthier approaches to emotional situations with his girlfriends. These repeated positive experiences can really help hone this skill set. In sum, it's a case of the rich getting richer. Now let's look at specifics. How does he respond to your needs?

Situation One: Bad Day

You've had a horrible day at work: your boss has intimated (not so subtly) that once again you've pissed off the not-so-likeable, yet integral person in the "important department" that you need to work cooperatively with to get some of your most significant work done. As you make your way home, you vacillate between self-doubt, self-loathing, high levels of frustration, and sheer contempt. Or maybe you've just had an awful fight with one of your closest friends. You never fought before and she is like a sister to you. You're feeling hurt, angry, and defensive for what you suspect your role may have been in the blowout.

The Optimal Response

The optimal response is characterized by one or more of the following: He listens to the whole story without interruptions. He lets you know he is tuned in by keeping up eye contact, not simultaneously doing something else such as taking apart the remote. He periodically utters "hmm" or nods (if you're not on the phone). He demonstrates recognition that you are unhappy, upset, angry, sad, and so on, by commenting to that effect. His statement may be a simple acknowledgment of your emotional state, for instance, "Wow, you look upset," or as advanced as a recognition of emotional state bound up with a shot of empathy: "I'm sorry you had to go through that." He makes a move to physically comfort you, but it's not sexual. He offers an opinion that is diplomatically stated in such a way as to tip the scales in your favor, from mildly to completely ("That's a tough situation. I guess she thought so and so, but I see your point completely" or "She is so unreasonable, you have every right to be totally pissed off").

Don't count on getting all of these requirements. To get them all is probably more like being with your therapist. To get a couple of them can be quite satisfying in the context of a relationship.

The Not-so-Good Response

The not-so-good response consists of some of the following: He rushes you along, interrupting with, "Yeah, but what happened?" He tells you he'll talk to you about it "later" and then never does. He moves immediately into problem-solving mode and starts interrupting with critiques of your behavior, in an aggressive play to turn down the heat of your emotion—all in the name of "helping you."

These are all escape/avoid tactics, and are indicative of a man who, for whatever reason, has the desire to move away from an emotionally charged conversation or a conversation about emotion. It's probably safe to say here that he has had bad experiences in this realm, both early on in childhood and more recently with his exes, and is trying to defend himself against yet another upsetting experience by either focusing on the intellectual aspects of the situation or trying to take hold of your feelings and quickly "cure" them by attempting to fix the problem and make it all go away.

This man likely had early experiences, with mom, sisters, and so on, and probably later experiences with his exes, that escalated and got out of control. It is possible that these women became inconsolable, hysterical, or turned their emotional struggle in his direction and lashed out at him with displaced anger. Whether in the victim or aggressor role, the mother-son dynamic here is one in which the son is often slammed with guilt for either causing or not being able to fix her pain. Now imagine how subconsciously anxious this guy may get at the mere sight of you in distress.

WHAT TO DO

Provided that you love this man and you want to try to make it work, remember that it does no one any good to let anger or upset get out of control. As Albert Ellis, the developer of Rational Emotive Behavior Therapy, put it, intense emotion is not the result of a situation; intense emotion happens in response to what one thinks or says to oneself about the situation. We're talking Anger Management 101 here, girls. Don't hold it in so long that you eventually explode like a firecracker, but don't explode on a regular basis either. Regular explosions are only practice for future explosions. Think about what is making you mad. Get clear on exactly what it is and put it into words. Describe it to him; don't take it out on him.

The same thing goes for managing your anxiety. Get a good handle on what's triggering your fears. Often times, anxious people are having vague thoughts about an overblown threat. Get a clear picture of yourself in these moments and have some compassion for him. Acknowledge that regular displays of intense emotion are probably only going to make him uncomfortable and lead him to withdraw. If he responds to your relatively tame, well-thought-out explanations over emotional explosions, you may have a guy who is capable of learning how to be there for you. If he continues to be avoidant, at least you have practiced more mature responses to stress that will likely help you in future relationships.

The Bad Response

He seems to listen, looks at you blankly, pauses, and then says "Well, yeah, but why are you so upset?" or, even, worse, "What should we do for dinner?" Or, he doesn't interrupt, but falls asleep instead.

Forget relationships with Mom and exes for the moment. This is the guy who is not good at reading body language/ facial expressions, or hearing tone of voice. He may pick up on the fact that something seems amiss, but it either doesn't register as important enough to check out or he doesn't know how to respond productively. Once he blunders several times and is then attacked or criticized or broken up with completely, he may become as defensive and avoidant as in the above scenarios.

Some men (and women, too) are just not as good at picking up on social cues, in spite of a loving relationship with a mother who set appropriate boundaries. Often, children with learning disabilities, attention deficit hyperactivity disorder (ADHD), or nonverbal learning disorders struggle with how to read and respond appropriately to more subtle social cues. Sometimes it just runs in families as acceptable behavior, displayed by parents and modeled by children.

WHAT TO DO

Of course, try and restrain an angry explosion by physically removing yourself from the situation for a short time. What can you do to navigate around it? You can vent to an understanding friend, or reframe by remembering that this is most likely not personal, but a situation requiring skills that are just not that developed in him. Most likely he does care, but is just not good at showing it. It should be noted here that if you are really convinced that he doesn't care, it's time to reconsider the whole relationship. As pointed out above, attacking in a fit of anger only serves to make someone become defensive and withdraw from you. In addition, this is one of those traits/deficits that you may have to turn the other cheek to. The question is, are there other qualities that endear him to you? Do you have the feeling that these are benevolent blunders without any malice? And do you have enough girlfriends to be there for you when he isn't giving you exactly what you need? If you answered yes, once again, practice using patience and look for additional solace elsewhere, and ask yourself some very key questions: Is he open to being taught? Does he make the effort, and know you don't expect him to change overnight? Is there enough good stuff to sustain you in general? Do you know how to be assertive about being attacked? Can you spread out your need for support to girlfriends, sisters, and Mom without an overdependence on him?

Situation Two: Bad Mood

A good, old-fashioned bad mood. All women get them, whether the underlying cause is PMS, lack of sleep, despair or frustration over an ongoing problem in the work or personal arenas, or just plain having woken up on the wrong side of the bed. You're snippy, curt, rude, moping, clingy, way-too-easily irritated, miserable, or predicting doom and death for all of mankind. And it's all happening on the day of his company picnic or a family get-together. Very likely an accident waiting to happen. How does he handle it?

The Optimal Response

He may try avoidance or empathy at first, but the best reaction here is that he stands up for himself by firmly letting you know that while whatever you're going through must be hard, you do not have the liberty to take your bad mood out on him and beat him up. In this scenario, he is not a milquetoast. You are responsible for controlling your bad mood and recognizing that, even if he is somehow involved in your dilemma, a tongue lashing just won't be productive.

An older man may be especially appreciative of, and impressed by, your insight and ability to admit a mistake.

The Not-so-Good Response

This can go in more than one direction. Too much empathy or doting, and you may feel as if you have a man who has no spine, and that's downright unattractive. Too much avoidance characterized by a cold shoulder is like passive aggression in response to, well, passive aggression. Instead of telling you in a calm, assertive way—or even with a hotheaded blow-up—he may let you know in an indirect, underhanded way by making snide remarks, huffing and puffing, and so on. Not a good recipe for love.

WHAT TO DO

For your own sake, it's important to recognize that if you find yourself becoming more aggressive in response to his reaction, this is not a behavior you want to keep on practicing. The same holds true for the passive-aggressive response. The cycle of indirectly hurting each other can last for a long time and do damage to each other and the relationship. Breaking out of a cycle like this requires that at least one of you confronts the problem in a more direct way by either asking to clear the air or initiating an apology. It is a bad situation if he is too easily baited and has no perspective on your mood, or too sensitive and takes it personally. It can be good if he gives *you* perspective on your mood and helps you realize you're stomping around like a baby.

The Bad Response

He responds to your bad mood by getting into an even blacker one. He begins to slam doors and stomp around; he

32

may begin to mutter and even flail his arms about. He may, in an ineffectual way, be trying to tell you that you are being childish, but he could lose control along the way.

WHAT TO DO

Sit down and think or write down in an organized way, all of your thoughts about what is bothering you and what you can possibly do about it. If you've already lashed out, acknowledge your mistake and accept the blame for your own bad mood. What to do here gets trickier, and if you find an ongoing pattern as described above, it may require the advice or guidance of a professional. You may need another person to help you sort out why your man would be frightened into doting on you when you are being a brat, and whether or not the extent of this dynamic crosses over into the realm of unhealthy behavior.

Situation Three: Tears

Crying. Yes, that's it in a word: crying. Never mind why, when, where, or who; there you are, sobbing your eyes out. This is a true litmus test for compassion, patience, and the ability to soothe and comfort. But beware, girls, the smart guy *will* bust you if you take advantage of this one.

The Optimal Response

He recognizes that you have broken down in response to hitting the limit of your stress or emotional level, and this is enough to make him feel concern and attempt to slow down what is going on. Active empathy is the best response and could be characterized by kind, understanding words or actions.

The Not-so-Good Response

He freezes like a deer in headlights and becomes remote. He doesn't want to know why you're crying and tries to hurry you out of it, again in the name of making you feel better.

WHAT TO DO
You will not be able to really teach him the complexity of response or the emotional freedom to feel and express empathy on the basis of nonverbal cues overnight. Patience here is extremely important. He may pick up the pointers and learn, or he may never excel at this sort of social code cracking. If you're happy enough with him in other ways, call your mother or your best friend when the tears are coming.

The Bad Response

He loses his temper and may even accuse you of being manipulative with your tears.

WHAT TO DO
You will have to carefully evaluate this situation. Be honest with yourself and consider the possibility that this could be grounds for ending your relationship. This kind of response to a loved one in emotional distress is likely to further the hurt and suffering you are feeling and is indicative of a man who has real difficulty putting himself in anyone else's shoes long enough to feel empathy for them. Watch out.

Situation Four: Name that Emotion

He's baffled by your sadness, bewildered because you're angry. He's honestly perplexed. When did these feelings start? Why didn't you just tell me? He asks, exasperated. One reason for his confusion may be that he is not reading the signs. Research shows that when it comes to facial expressions that reflect the more complex and subtle emotional states, men don't read faces as well as women.

The Optimal Response

He does not get upset with you; in fact, he tries diplomatically to get you to talk about whatever it is that is bothering you. He knows that "fine" is just a put-off, but doesn't come back with the same attitude. The understanding approach is highly refined; often only the Wise Guy has fully mastered it. He gives you space, but lets you know that when you want to talk, he'll be there for you; and if you want to handle it on your own, he'll respect that, too.

The Not-so-Good Response

He makes one try, then tells you to "tough it out." Or he may just tell you to keep crying and "get if off your chest."

WHAT TO DO
Explain to him that his being attentive at this moment will not make it last longer. Quite the opposite, it will help you recover more quickly. His coach-like advice would be more helpful if he warmed it up a bit, too ("Cry all you need babe, get it all out, I'm here for you" and "You are tough, you are a survivor, you'll get through this").

The Bad Response

He wants to know *what* you're pissed off about, not why. Or he may personalize it immediately and come out with:

"Now what have I done?" He gets caught up in your anger and thinks a confrontation will clear the air.

In both these responses, watch out if his reaction to sadness or fear is anger and a desire to fight.

WHAT TO DO

If he's willing to have the discussion, you'll need to repeat that he need not take every frown or twitch personally. This guy obviously has a past when it comes to distressed women. Finding out about it in order to emphasize how you are different is your goal. It might help him to know that you do not always handle emotional issues in the best way and also that you have to learn to communicate more effectively.

Situation Five: We Need to Talk

This is a hair-raising, stomach-sinking statement for a number of men. How many times has he heard this? Has he learned from the more patient and articulate women in his past that relationships are living entities that are dynamic in nature and need ongoing input (in the form of communication, mutual respect, and having some downright good times together) in order to flourish? Or is this a guy who's been subjected to the "You're getting an overhaul, buster, or I'm out the door" a million times. So, when you say this to your older man, how does he respond?

The Optimal Response

When you say, "we need to talk," the optimal response would be one that invites dialogue, something like "Of course, honey; what's on your mind?" When women say, "We need to talk," it means they want to sit down and address an ongoing problem or check out a potential one. Often, they are asking for the specifics about the required amount of time and effort that should be put into the relationship.

The Not-so-Good Response

If he begins to back himself into a corner and asks you "*Now* what have I done?" you know that he automatically responds on the defensive. It then turns into a battle of wills—he immediately puts himself on the other side of the ring rather than in a team or problem-solving mode.

WHAT TO DO

When he hears the dreaded four word sentence, his gut reaction is often, "Why is she analyzing every move I make and every word that comes out of my mouth, when all I did was walk in the door after a hard day at work, or when all I wanted to know is if she ate lunch?" Try to explain with great patience and tact that what comes naturally to women, may be seen by him as unnecessary at best, or an attack in the worst-case scenario. Explain that you are not attacking him, and that you know that you, too, are a fallible, imperfect human, but that you are just trying to nip a potential problem (or an ongoing one) in the bud.

The Bad Response

Total avoidance. He heads for the door, gets in the car, and burns rubber leaving the driveway. For him, "We have to talk" is a prelude to a break-up.

WHAT TO DO

Make sure he is not feeling smothered or threatened. Women can go over a situation time and time again, each

Dating the Older Man

time examining a different angle or interpretation. Young women have a tendency to overanalyze every aspect of a relationship (what he said, what I said, what he might have said, what I didn't say). For women it is leisurely and pleasurable to get on the phone and analyze guys and their behavior with their friends. Men do not enjoy this activity. They are not wired for it and it is taxing on them. Then again, there has to be a minimum of contact and communication. Watch out if you feel lonely or apart too often. Molehills can easily turn into mountains.

Situation Six: How Do I Look?

Ultimately, how you feel about your overall self and your looks is what matters, and when you feel good, you're much more resilient to life's hard knocks. Expecting your boyfriend (or anyone else for that matter) to create and maintain your self-esteem is like trying to fill a lake with a squirtgun—it's not happening. That's your job. But, hey, it's nice to know that you are attractive to your man, and it's perfectly healthy to want to feel that way.

For him, your asking of his opinion on how you look is a Catch-22 if there ever was one. After all, some women do not want to be patronized, some want to hear a good fat, juicy lie once in a while, and probably all women want some combination of the two, but who in the world really knows how to read feminine minds with 100 percent accuracy?

The Good Response

The best is hearing that you're beautiful and sexy no matter what you're wearing, and said with gusto. Of course, the ultimate response would be some added detail, a comment on the color that enhances your complexion, the style that flatters your figure, the type of material that flows so beautifully with your walk. But that really is the ultimate response, and you should only expect that from dear female friends.

The Not-so-Good Response

As long as you get some approximation of "You are beautiful in my eyes no matter how much of a wreck you look like," delivered in a nonjudgmental tone, he has met the very basic requirements. Beware of the sugar-coated opinion: He may be trying to squirm out of being truthful or hoping to avoid what he fears will be a long, drawn-out discussion.

WHAT TO DO

We have to confess that we feel for the man who is asked this question, and would say that he's got to be allowed to blunder his way through this one with utter impunity— with one caveat. Specifically, the words he uses to craft his answer and the tone of voice he uses to deliver them. After all, research shows that people respond more to tone of voice than choice of words. With tact, you can help him through this one, but since it's not a life-or-death situation, go easy on the guy and trust yourself and the mirror.

The Bad Response

The worst scenario here would be that he gives a raw opinion and runs away. If he shrugs his shoulders and asks why you're asking him, of all people, or reminds you of the last time his opinion was disregarded, be careful—he's been burned before.

WHAT TO DO

If you don't get the response you want, your guy should not be tortured with crying, sulking, pouting, or changing into ten different outfits. Men are not used to giving detailed critiques of women's clothing (in fact, they usually agree that naked is the best outfit). Or, on the other hand, if he is too critical and pressures you too much to look a certain way, you really do have to evaluate the relationship: Is he trying to remake you in an ex's image?

Situation Seven: Do You Know What Today Is?

He forgets your birthday, your anniversary. Everyone wants to be remembered on birthdays and anniversaries. In the grand scheme of things, however, you need to ask yourself how important this one really is—especially if you feel happy on the other 364 days.

The Optimal Response

He knows what day it is, and whips out a present from behind his back.

The Not-so-Good Response

He remembers at least most of the time, and promises to get you a gift.

WHAT TO DO

Drop a hint when you're nearing a date that is important to you. Or easier still, write it on the calendar on refrigerator door in a red magic marker. Don't test the poor guy to see if he actually follows up with a gift; just point and smile when you see it next time you are out.

The Bad Response

He forgets and then tries to trivialize these events as silly opportunities for you to ask for a present.

WHAT TO DO

If you feel loved overall, try, try, try not to take this one personally when faced with the last two responses. If he forgets your anniversary, you be the bigger one and call him up and present him with a gift without getting angry or accusatory and he'll likely feel like responding in kind. If that fails, have him program the dates with a beeping alarm on his BlackBerry. If that fails, you may just have to make the reservation and get the present yourself. At this stage of the game, this is one battle you might want to put down at the bottom of your list.

Situation Eight:
Girls' Night Out/Boys' Night Out

Girls just want to have fun, and so do guys. The poet Khalil Gibran speaks of how separateness in relationships is required in order for there to be true togetherness. In other words, you need to be an individual with time to yourself in order to be a functional part of a healthy couple, and so does he. It's a great feeling to be able to break away and go out with friends without worrying that he'll feel neglected or paranoid. That way you can feel really free to enjoy your time with others and to experience yourself as a separate person, an individual outside of the couple. Here's your chance to see movies, try restaurants, and experience things that he doesn't enjoy.

The Optimal Response

With his experience and practice, he probably realizes the importance of time out without each other. In this best case scenario, he wishes you a good night out and then shows he means it by not giving you any grief for it after the fact.

The Not-so-Good Response

The controlling, paranoid response is to make it difficult for you to break away for fun with friends. He may not trust you, or he just may not be able to deal with being alone himself. Whatever the case, there is guilt and tension around your wanting to go out, and it can deeply impact your feelings about him in a negative way.

When it comes to his turn, he may not be in the habit of calling and may be in the habit of disappearing for a long night out. If that's the case, again it's a matter of deciding how much you can put up with. Remember, this pattern of taking off for the night is probably a well-worn habit developed in past relationships or in someone who has been a chronic bachelor. For him, having to stay in contact is akin to feeling as if he has to report to his mommy.

WHAT TO DO

If you trust him and know that he, like the entire male species, needs to just go off and be with the guys every once in awhile, don't give him grief. Try to be gracious when it's clear that he'd like to do something with his friends. It's sometimes okay and even helpful to ask up front if he'd like to be together on any given night or hang out with his friends. But do ask him to call you and let you know he'll be extra late. On your end, if you know you're going to be really late, call.

Other strategies to cope with the desire for time apart include scheduling regular time to do what you both like, having friends in common to do things with, and having your or his close friends join you more often to become more comfortable with each other.

The Bad Response

A bad response to this situation would be an extreme version of the not-so-good response, and you will have to be wary of this one. Being controlled and kept in an invisible cage is totally unhealthy and something to avoid. If either one of you is plagued by intense fears of abandonment, is extremely possessive, and literally can't let your significant other out of your sight, beware.

What to do: If you find that you feel you need all of his time or vice versa, think seriously about getting some professional help. While in the beginning that protectiveness was playful, one of you is now tiptoeing around, lying in order to see your friends—and it's only going to get worse without intervention. That poet was right: If you want real togetherness you have to be able to be apart sometimes.

Situation Nine: I Don't Feel So Good . . .

There's a reason that wedding vows include "in sickness and in health"—couples respond very differently to each other when one is ill. What happens when you are the one who needs nursing or mothering for the flu, a broken bone, or a simple stomachache?

The Optimal Response

Assuming you don't constantly have an ailment (think "the boy who cried wolf"), he acknowledges your discomfort sympathetically and offers to buy cough syrup or chicken soup.

The Not-so-Good or Bad Response

He tells you to "suck it up" or ignores you altogether. As one woman put it, "Unless blood is pouring out of some wound or orifice, he has no clue that I could be feeling too ill to get everything accomplished in my day."

WHAT TO DO

This is a tough one, and you may never get the empathic, care-taking response you are looking for, but you have to set limits when it comes to your health. In other words, it is necessary to make time for yourself to rest and get better without his blessing or permission.

Situation Ten: My Ex This and My Ex That

Maybe he's a guy who "hangs on to things" or maybe it's just that he spent so much time with one woman that he's not used to being with someone new and has only that one reference point. Photos of them in happier times may be around his place and he may like to frequent their old haunts. In this case it is very possible that starting fresh means abandoning his memories, which can be akin to losing his very identity. It can be very difficult for an older man who has been in a very long marriage or relationship to make the change to a new environment, a new girlfriend, new music, a new life, and what feels like a new self. You've asked nicely and . . .

The Optimal Response

He acknowledges your point, recognizes your feelings about it, and makes efforts to put reminders of the past away. Moving forward, you notice fewer references to the ex.

The Not-so-Good Response

He may not come out and say it, but by his actions it's clear that this is difficult for him. In short, he's clinging to his old life for too long into your relationship. What's too long? It's been six months to a year and not only does he still have old photos displayed, but he's also asking you to make her meatloaf recipe.

WHAT TO DO

The best-case scenario is that you trust him and feel loved enough to let him have visible reminders of the continuity of his life from his ex-wife's chapter to yours. Don't expect him to act as if that chapter of his life never happened—that's not fair. Beyond that, explain that it feels uncomfortable and that you'd appreciate it if he'd put certain photos away. Make sure you also are surrounded with beautiful photos of the two of you in the present for balance!

The Bad Response

He says it's out of the question and accuses you of jealousy.

WHAT TO DO

You may have to seek professional help because this is definitely an extreme response. You can try to sit down and talk it out, but if that doesn't work and he won't accept some sort of counseling, you may have to consider walking away.

Laugh Together, Admire Each Other

There you have it: what we feel are the most common, most obvious older man traits and tough situations. While this is admittedly a general guide, there are basic ideas that can be quite useful in most relationship scenarios. Just remember that, regardless of age, you need to be able to communicate effectively with your older man. If you think it's tough now, wait until you are negotiating for higher stakes about things such as children and retirement plans. If you have the ability to laugh together and respect and admire one another (not to mention good sex), you stand a better chance of weathering the tough times.

three

Friends and Foes

One of the first things people do when they meet someone who is a potential friend, coworker, or family member by marriage is to look hard for similarities. In a younger-woman/older-man scenario, the first thing your friends will probably notice is a bunch of differences. He's unlike the guys you've dated before, unlike your friends, and unlike you! Don't be surprised or hurt if numerous friends bristle or, at least, show concern. Given the age difference they see, they may feel worried about you, confused by your choice, afraid that this relationship will change you and your friendship, or even jealous.

Be aware that some of their negative anticipations may stem from love—clearly they don't want to see you being used or getting hurt. But there is a big difference between being protective of a beloved friend and being close-minded and rude. On the other hand, it may be your older boyfriend's behavior that is out of line, and he may be the one who needs the "talking to" instead of them. By the same token, dealing with his friends may be just as hard, or harder, than negotiating all this with your buddies, especially when you have no history with them and you're not even sure you like them. This chapter will help sort out all those dynamics: the good, the bad, and the ugly.

In Her Words

"I've always mixed with people older than me. I'm often told I appeal to older men more than to guys my own age, and I think that's pretty cool. Older men understand women more. They usually have better taste."

Scarlett Johansson

If your friends dislike your older man, try to consider the possibility that their reasons are justified. Behaving like a fraud, an egomaniac, a control freak, a cheat, or a bore, are all good reasons not to like the guy; his graduating from high school when you were still in diapers is not!

Introduction Jitters

Whether it's sooner or later, the importance of friends and the roles they play in each of your lives will come up as a topic of conversation and an issue to be assessed with greater precision. Men we interviewed in focus groups and in therapy realized that how they were received by their girlfriend's friends—involving the obvious and unwritten social expectations and ongoing dynamics with her friends—was not only a hot topic of discussion but a real obstacle to overcome and master. Many sensitive older men walk into new situations with genuine trepidation, wanting to please and wearing their hearts on their sleeves, as shown in the following examples.

"Over the years I have brought several of the women I dated to meet my friends. They are used to the fact that I date. They've set me up and seen women come and go. The only thing I wanted to make sure is that they understood Kathy was going to be around for a while, not just for one barbecue or dinner party."—Clarke, 37

"Elizabeth was the first woman I had brought to meet my friends. All the others I had dated, I'd met theirs from time to time, but I felt like Elizabeth should meet mine. I was nervous about how they'd respond to her. She is pretty, but apart from that, she is intelligent and funny, I hoped they'd see that, too."—Ben, 42

"Though I'd been divorced for about two years, my friends and my ex-wife knew each other. It was hard being around them and for her name not to come up in some way. I'm sure they'd compare Felicia to her, how she looked, what she did for a living, how she acted around me. And more so, how I acted around her. Holly, my ex, had started dating right away. I had taken a little longer."—Shawn, 51

"While with Abbey, we'd go out with a group of people; with my friends, it was either events or dinners with another couple. The vibes were different."—Patrick, 58

So you see, in the hopes and fears department, it's not very different for women, who come to learn that expectations are different, and at times, unpredictable.

"I had married a very successful and controlling doctor my age but after we divorced, I started dating a guy ten years my senior who was a landscaper. There's no doubt

I picked someone who is completely opposite from my ex for a reason. I knew when I met his friends they would want to see if I was down-to-earth enough for them, and that I wouldn't judge them for not being professionals with a lot of money."—Lindsay, 38

"Despite our age difference, Paul and I did exactly the same thing at work. We met at the office and could spend hours talking about trends and analysis, each keeping the other up on research and latest news. We were equals when it came to money. I wanted to make sure his circle of friends knew that."—Jennifer, 43

"I took off two years before going to college, took five years to graduate, and then interned for a year. At twenty-eight, I had a job that was in the field I wanted, but made just barely enough to pay my rent and eat. The fact that Larry had money and would rather spend it on making my life easier so I could spend time with him, and be relaxed when I was with him, made a huge difference for both of us. I liked him and his being generous was icing on the cake. I'm sure his couples friends figured this out, but I still tried not to let it bother me."—Sue, 28

Will Their Opinions Change
When They Actually See You Happy?

One of the main things your friends will ask (or hint at) is, "Why him?" Or, "Why an older guy, period?" One of the best answers: He is happy and he makes me happy. Lots of women are tired of dating unhappy, immature, cynical men who don't know how to control their tempers and haven't found themselves. Many older men have been through this kind of personal development, and the relatively lower levels of testosterone typical of older men can truly help them be less hotheaded, and, consequently, better analytical thinkers. Typically, men are looking for happiness and acceptance in a woman and can be very grateful and appreciative when they find it. Laura Cartensen, a psychology professor and aging specialist, writes in an article titled "At The Intersection of Emotion and Cognition: Aging and the Positivity Effect": "How often one feels sad, angry, disgusted, contemptuous— that frequency declines. And in addition to that, when negative emotions occur, they don't last as long."

> ❧ Experts say the number of people ending long-term marriages after age fifty is steadily increasing. Few states include age in their divorce statistics, but researchers—and those involved in divorce filings—say the trend is clear. "So many of this generation are sitting with the prospect of many happy, healthy years ahead of them," says Kate Vetrano, chair of the Elder Law Committee of the Family Law Section of the American Bar Association. "They're shedding their marriages in the quest for happiness."

Friends Behaving Badly

A little fuzzy on when your friends' behavior crosses the line? If a friend's curiosity or questioning makes you feel hurt or embarrassed, before you jump the gun and blame them for their insensitivity, ask yourself if it's something you already feel ashamed of or weird about. If so, you can accuse them of being clumsy in their approach to finding out about your life, but you can't accuse them of having bad or hurtful intentions. Big difference. If they're good friends and you have a history with them characterized by support and care, try and give them the benefit of the doubt. We'll speak about handling a confrontation later in the chapter.

Below are some typical questions any friend would ask, with or without finesse. Circle the comments in the following chart that best describe your friends' behavior. If you've been asked any of them and have some answers in the inappropriate column, you may need to have a sit down with your friend and make it clear that it can hurt to have someone show interest in your relationship as if she were a spectator at the circus.

Appropriate	Inappropriate
What does he do for a living?	How much money does he make?
Where did you two meet?	Why isn't he married to someone his own age?
I'm happy that you're happy.	Why? *Why*?
So, how's the sex?	Does he take Viagra?
Does he have any kids?	Do you really want to be a stepmother?

My BFFs

If a rift occurs between you and your friends, you have to consider the possibility that he might be to blame. If your older man belittles your friends' opinions, talks down to them, or has a way of making your friends feel as if they're in the presence of a Nobel Prize–winner just because he's got a few extra years on them, you may need to sit him down and talk about his social etiquette with your friends. Interaction with friends can be a great litmus test for just how wonderful your wonderful boyfriend's character really is.

Again, circle the comments in the following chart that best describe his behavior and go from there.

Appropriate	Inappropriate
I was actually around when that happened.	You wouldn't understand what I'm talking about.
That's an interesting point.	That's something my daughter would say.
I have to get going—1 A.M. is my limit on a Tuesday night.	Don't you girls have to get up in the morning?
Your friends are nice.	Wow, Jeanine is hot!
I disagree with what you're saying.	When you get to be my age, you'll understand.
Baby, you're beautiful.	By the time you're that age it won't even matter to me. Besides, the holidays are coming and plastic surgery would make a great gift.

Uncomfortable Friends

They are going to have a reaction to his age, whether it will be good, bad, wary, or amused. It may be a hurdle for you to address, or you might have to just sit it out until the dust settles.

But I'll Get in Trouble . . .

Your best friend Megan swears like a truck driver, but upon meeting your older man, she only slips once and apologizes to him when she does. In the not-so-far-back of your mind you know why: He reminds her of her dad, or her grammar school principal, or maybe even her church priest. You wonder if he noticed and hope that someday soon she'll relax and eventually go back to the potty-mouth self you love her for. If your friends start "behaving" because somehow his age or demeanor inspires guilt in them, you might consider modeling the at-times-goofy or irreverent behavior they are accustomed to in order to show them he won't ground them or make them sit on the bench.

Leveling the Playing Field

You introduce your older man (a senior financial analyst) to your work pal Greg (a graphic artist) for the first time at a dinner party. In an attempt to make your OM more comfortable, Greg gropes for topics that seem age-appropriate, like how the Dow Jones responded to the Fed's cut in interest rates, something he himself barely understands, let alone wants to sit there and talk about in detail. But being the good friend that he is, Greg is trying in earnest to level the playing field. Unbeknownst to Greg, however, OM is very worldly, experienced, and hip enough to sit there and chat about a wide variety of topics they can relate to in spite of the age difference. You end up thanking Greg profusely for trying his best to sound like a fifty-year old on your behalf, and you end up apologizing to your OM, who is a good sport and kids around, playfully mimicking Greg's strained efforts to talk about international finance and the *Billboard* top hits in 1958. Try using your knowledge that they both like *Seinfeld*, author Robert Ludlum, or chess to bridge the conversation until it comes naturally.

When the OM Doesn't Measure Up to the YM in Your Friends' Eyes

Your same-aged ex blended right in with your friends and even kept some of them for himself after you broke up, yet your friends treat your OM like a visitor. After you broke up with your YM, they were all so upset. It's like they had to break up with him, too, and now you're having to deal with another (much older) guy filling those shoes. Getting together as a group was so easy before and now it's double the work. You are hoping that eventually the group will accept OM for himself and that you can go back to enjoying nights out with the group as you did before.

How to Cope When Fear of Friend Rejection Grips You

With all of this change and novelty in your social and romantic life, don't feel surprised if you vacillate and doubt your own feelings. Your friends are just being themselves but you find yourself tense, hoping they won't be too juvenile in front of him. Are his clothes too formal or even frumpy? Worse, is he trying too hard to look young? You watch your own reactions; maybe you stay by his side feeling as if you need to protect him. Maybe you watch his every move to see how much he is trying (after all, your friends hopefully mean something to him because they're, well, your friends), and hoping his efforts are effective.

The day after you finally introduce your OM to your friends, you brace yourself for their reactions in private. Will they avoid the topic all together? Ask in a crude way how it feels to be with a man that age in bed? Exclude you from events because you are all grown up now (regardless of your age)? The answer really depends on what kind of friends they are.

The Good Friend

The simple fact here is that a good friend will stick by you and not judge you. A good friend will be happy for you if you seem to be genuinely happy. By the same token, a good friend will watch your back and point out things she thinks are not good for you. How she communicates, and when she chooses to tell you what's on her mind, matter a lot. It's easy to get along with articulate friends who know how to word things appropriately or who are good at sensing how far to go with their questioning. It's much harder to relate to a friend who is being too critical, too nosy, or suddenly distant.

> ᔢ It helps a lot to start off with a positive statement first. (e.g., "I really appreciate you coming out to dinner," or "you know I love you but"). Then make "I" statements such as "when X happened I felt . . ." Also, if it's a good friend, don't be afraid to admit some of your own insecurities and take ownership of them (e.g., "I know you were only kidding about X but you hurt my feelings").

One really important thing to keep in mind is the track record you have with this friend. If you have trust and the gut feeling that this friend really cares for you, cut her some slack. Keep your temper in check and be direct.

The Frenemy

Most of us encountered our first friend/enemy hybrid in an eighth-grade classroom, but she also grows up (notice we did not say matures), and walks this earth as a twenty-, thirty-, or forty-something. She's the kind of person who often plays the game of "one-up-man-ship," which is the equivalent of outdoing anyone in any act or even conversation. This person typically has low self-esteem and is easily threatened by the achievements or accomplishments of peers—which is exactly how she may view your relationship: as a big accomplishment. She either runs in the same circles or works with you, so you are stuck with her.

To her, you may have just hit the jackpot for life and she's jealous. Do not get sucked into any kind of dispute with this person, nor play her game of doing you one better in conversation. The best thing to do here is fly under the radar. If you see her out socially, just keep your happiness and the fun you are having to yourself. By the same token, don't cry miserably in front of her either. Anything you say can and will be used against you at some point, so keep it neutral and save the juicy details for a friend who has the capacity to be genuinely happy for you.

Dealing with Distance

The most common reaction friends might have to your new relationship is to put distance between you. Good friends or not, they are who they are and they may just have their own personal reasons for feeling uncomfortable around him. By all means try to maintain the friendship and do things with these friends on your own. Also, check yourself: Is your conversation about him always about things they can't relate to? Do you talk about him and stress how different he was from your other boyfriends (the same ones they continue to date)? Be sure to keep on being a good listener for them, and just as you don't want to be judged for choosing an OM, don't judge them when they're telling you their woes about dating a peer.

Three Steps to Artful Confrontation

When introducing your OM to your friends, you may find yourself disappointed by your friends' actions or comments. So, how do you react without destroying your friendship? There is a saying that we consider some of the best advice we've ever heard: "Right at the time when you feel you must speak, the smartest thing to do is keep your mouth shut." If you are chomping at the bit to open your mouth, chances are you are fully charged with an emotion that hasn't been thoroughly processed by the intellectual part of your brain. When you feel hurt or angry by a comment or an action, the hardest and always best thing to do is sit back and give it time to sink in. The way you think about what happened is also critical at this moment.

> ✿ The best way to respond to a hurtful comment or action is to calmly make an "I hurt" statement, such as "I felt really hurt and embarrassed when you and Sarah snickered in the corner and didn't introduce yourselves to Tim when we showed up at the restaurant." Then listen; she may have a good reason for her behavior that has nothing to do with you. If you are serious about your older man, you need to make it clear that he really matters to you and you would appreciate that they be as supportive as possible.

If you continuously re-indoctrinate yourself with your own hurt, angry perspective by saying, for example: "I can't believe how insensitive/cruel/mean she is," you will be limiting yourself. Let her opinions sink in and give thought to her perspective and then ask yourself why she did or said what she did. That is not making excuses for your friend or giving her a free pass; it's getting perspective or a true understanding of what actually happened. Also, think about *why* her comments or actions hurt you. Are you overly sensitive on this issue or has this been a pattern of insensitive behavior on your friend's part for as long as you can recall? Once you feel as if you have a decent understanding of your hurt feelings and your friend's possible motives, think about how you would like someone to admit their hurt or anger to you if you were the one who had committed the transgression.

Real-Life Friend Scenarios and How to Cope

The reality is that your OM is not going to fit in as perfectly as your same-age friends. He might find a connection with one or two in particular due to special interests, but the dynamic of your relationship with your friends and your new relationships is going to be more challenging and different than ever before.

The worst-case scenario is that your friends don't like him or vice versa. The heart of the matter is that you like him, you are keeping him, and everyone around you is just going to have to deal with it. On the flip side, your friends and family have been around forever, and, as a result, he has to accept the fact that they are a part of your life, and in turn, his life as well. Here are some rules for a variety of scenarios that will help you keep the peace so they can all get along, and maybe, eventually, they will actually come to like each other.

Scenario One: Friends Are Lukewarm

They aren't hostile, but definitely not warm and welcoming. Maybe they liked your ex more, or maybe he reminds them of their silver-haired stepfathers. . . .

Your Reaction: You vacillate between feeling protective of him and feeling fearful that you may lose your friends. Will they stop calling you?

What you shouldn't do: Force them together.

What you should do: Make sure that when they do hang out, it is in the best setting possible—either a neutral setting or a place they both like. Both your friends and your OM should know that their getting along is really important to you. Tell them how much you appreciate their making an effort.

Troubleshoot: Don't take him to everything. Make sure you continue to spend one-on-one time with your friends. They figure they were there before him and probably will be there long after he's gone.

Scenario Two: They Hate Each Other

Or they like him but he hates them; or vice versa.

Your Reaction: You are saddened and maybe angry at their refusal or inability to be happy for you and recognize how happy you are.

What you shouldn't do: Hold court and have everyone explain their dislikes. Or separate the two, having only friends' time and only OM time. This will drive you nuts since you'll also find you can't talk about one to the other without each getting a snarl on their face or a look of exasperated boredom.

Troubleshoot: Let each party know you understand their feelings but make it clear to both that you will choose your boyfriends and you will choose your friends and that if they all care about you, they'll bite the bullet and be polite. If you have an OM or a friend on your hands who cannot rein in his or her obnoxious or aggressive behavior, something isn't right. The smartest thing to do is ask yourself if they are making positive contributions to your life or if you would be better off without them.

Scenario Three: They Are Suspicious of Each Other

He wonders: Will they convince her we are not good for each other?

They ask: Will he take her away and turn her into someone we no longer recognize?

Your Reaction: Healthy suspicion and being protective is nice; anything more than that is infantilizing you. You are a big girl now.

What you shouldn't do: Try to eradicate this normal emotion too quickly by talking it to death with your friends.

What you should do: Keep being happy and peaceful. They will look to see how you are reacting as a barometer of how good he is to you. Eventually your continued happiness should outweigh initial fears or opinions.

Troubleshoot: While you need to vent, be careful to whom you vent since they are already on high alert. You can rev your friend up into a rip roaring frenzy at him, but being "in love" means that you can bounce right back. Friends can't do that but they can store up tales of how mean or insensitive he's been. So while you might get over it quickly and go back to him, they may not be able to cool down so fast. Friends who have a lot of relationship experience will understand this whole rollercoaster ride better, so vent to someone with experience.

Scenario Four: Your Friends Do a Double-Take

"That's her boyfriend?" Maybe your friends know he's older, but they're not sure how much older, until a date slips out in conversation. Then you see them do the math silently and raise an eyebrow or two.

Your Reaction: It can be anything from nervousness and confusion to anger.

What you shouldn't do: You shouldn't begin to rationalize the age difference or stress how many things you do together. Do not try to convince them. Nor should you become angry and stiff at the dinner table.

What you should do: Gradually introduce him to your close friends in the most intimate settings possible, and in group settings for the others. If they are uncomfortable, give them all time. Once they get used to each other, provided they get along fairly well, it should not be an issue that everyone is pointing at. Don't get paranoid; this will only bring more attention to the situation. Stay calm and have a good time; there will be plenty of other things to focus on which will certainly take the spotlight off you guys.

Troubleshoot: Keep cool. You want them to like him, and you want him to like them, too, so act as normally as you can. This maximizes the potential for a positive outcome and your friends will begin to take him in stride and not gawk.

HIS TAKE ON THE WHOLE FRIENDS SITUATION?

- He likes you, so if you have to get together from time to time with them, he is a gentleman about it.
- He has no trouble fitting in with your friends and can hold conversations with them about anything. He asks questions and genuinely seems interested.
- He has kids that easily could have attended your friends' parties, yet he doesn't act like a father or childish.
- He feels threatened by your friends, as if they might make fun of him and introduce you to some young hunk who will take you away.
- He can't believe you actually get along with these people, and though he doesn't say so straight out, you can tell he is relieved to leave.

It's a great thing to have your new guy tell you he thinks your best friends are great. He sees what you love about them. It's just as great to receive a phone call from your closest friends commenting on how witty, handsome, and interesting your new OM seems. While this doesn't happen all the time, you can hope they will grow on each other. If your OM's or friends' behavior really crosses the line, you can question your choice of friends or mate. You can also just accept the fact that not all people in your life are going to like each other. Then let them deal with it; it doesn't have to be your match to referee.

SOME RULES TO KEEP EVERYONE AS HAPPY AS POSSIBLE

1. Though you may be doing different things with your new guy, make time to see your friends. Don't call them only when you two are not getting along.
2. While you can talk about him as frequently as you would any boyfriend, try to focus less on his age and more on the dynamic. It will give your friends topics of conversation to be able to share, rather than feel like it's a situation they don't know anything about.
3. Don't force him on them or them on him—even if you desperately want them to like each other. Don't keep giving him or them reasons why the other party is "great." Let them discover each other on their own.
4. Remember that getting used to a new person takes a while. He needs to see how well they treat you and vice versa.
5. Do not lose your sense of humor. As long as it's playful and not hurtful, let yourself laugh at the situation with both parties.

Meeting His Friends

"Paul showed up beaming with his new girlfriend. She looked like my little sister. Just the sight of her annoyed me. She giggled and clung to his every word."

"Though I had heard she was fifteen years his junior, they looked pretty good together. Andy had lost some weight and if I didn't know, I wouldn't have guessed at the age difference."

"Terrence was lonely and had money to burn. While part of me was annoyed knowing she was letting him pay for things, the other part of me thought, as long as you are sweet to him, that's okay. He is a good guy."

Reactions can be mixed and unexpected. His female friends, or wives of male friends, can look at you in several ways, either through rose-colored glasses or suspiciously. They are probably checking you out and thinking one of the following:

- He's dating. Big deal.
- This is one of the women he dates.
- I'll be pleasant. Eventually she'll go away.
- He looks so happy.
- She seems fairly normal even though she is significantly younger.
- Let's give her a chance and see what she is made of.
- She is the polar opposite of his ex-wife; he is obviously only going out with her as a reaction to the divorce.
- She is going to get tired of him and leave him. I wish I could warn him.
- She obviously is around for the ride.
- I'm sure she is completely vapid.

And the worst one:

- Is this what will happen if my husband and I ever break up? She'll probably set him up with one of her friends!

In Her Words

"Oh, you are the one who does hair," was the first reaction I got from one of the wives of his friends. "Actually I do hair and makeup for television," I tried nicely to convey. She later introduced me as a hairdresser again. I wanted to yell at her: "Sure I cut hair; I also styled it, did makeup, and made good money working on set at different theaters and television sets." But she didn't want to hear it. His female friends and buddies' wives wanted to keep thinking that I was in it for the meal ticket. I wasn't. I had no intention of leaving my job; it had taken me a long time to get to where I was and I loved it. "

Jennifer, 40

HIS FRIENDS: SOUND FAMILIAR?

The Open-Minded Friend: He or she is happy to meet you and treats you as if they are meeting someone interesting who likes their friend. He treats you as if you already have something in common—which you do! He asks you questions, real questions, about you, your job, your family. Whenever you see them at a gathering, you feel relieved.

The Friend of the Wife/or Ex (wife or girlfriend) who put him through school: She makes sure that you know that you are reaping what someone else sowed. She wants to be sure that you appreciate withdrawing savings that someone else deposited.

The Protector: This person wants to be assured that you will take care of your older man. He or she is slow to warm up and asks questions about your plans to see where your OM fits in, and asks a lot of background questions. This person makes you feel like asking, "Did I get the job?" Don't fret—this person often relaxes significantly once you've jumped through a few hoops.

The Skeptic: He asks questions that verge on the inappropriate. He almost comes out and asks if you really know "what you are getting in for" and offers several examples of May-December couples that didn't make it.

The Insecure Wife: Worries out loud about her looks; asks you several times how old you think she is. Is continually looking for her husband and talking about how many things they did together and how perfect they are for each other.

The Chop Buster: Teases you to the point of pissing you off, then eases back. Then starts again and eases off. Later calls you a good sport.

This whole process can help you define more clearly who you are in regards to what you will and won't tolerate. It can be emotionally draining at times, and during much of the first part of the relationship you may find yourself questioning your own feelings and mulling over such existential themes as the true meaning of love, friendship, and death. Use this time to answer soul-searching questions:

- Is there a difference between what friendship means to you and to him?
- Is there something you are embarrassed about or that you are particularly sensitive to that came up when you met his friends?

- Is there something that you feel you missed out on or have to give up to get along with his friends?

What Is His Role?

When it comes to the part he will play in your life, significant questions to ponder are: When does he need to step in and tell his friends either to back off or try to be warmer with you? When are remarks crossing the line from catty to insulting?

While you may omit your reactions to some of the more difficult nuances of the evening from him, deciding when to let him step in or when to tell him how you are being treated when he goes to the bar to get more drinks is a sensitive topic. Best rules: Don't react immediately; take some time to simmer down so you have perspective. Try to foresee what telling him will do to his friendship and your relationship. Watching his reaction—be it supportive, thoughtful, explosive, suspicious, or dismissive and avoidant—offers valuable information and is predictive of what you can most likely continue to expect.

Just when you've conquered your social circle with him as your partner, it may be time to meet the family. Don't be pessimistic, but know that you have some preparing to do. You now have some experience under your belt—and chances are, you'll need it.

four

Meet the Family

You can bank on the idea that your parents won't be 100 percent supportive of the fact that your new boyfriend was a rookie when your father was captain of the high school football team. Somehow team spirit doesn't help this time. After all, they are your parents and part of their mission in life is to protect you from all the scary, offensive, and harmful elements in this world. If you have conservative parents, you can expect them to have some objections to what, in their eyes, is a nontraditional union at best and a downright foolish choice at worst.

One primary concern a lot of parents may have is how the two of you will age together. What will happen when he really starts to get older, when he's well into his seventies and eighties and you're itching to travel the world? Or worse, he passes away while you're still alive and well?

Unlike some of your more beat-around-the-bush friends, many parents will feel comfortable enough to tackle the subject early on. Then again, if you've been the rebellious type, they probably don't want to push you into his arms by being harshly critical and putting you on the defensive. So how they make their points may be more subtle. How can you tell if they're less than pleased?

In Her Words

"Joe is nine years older and looks it. I was actually relieved it was only nine; I thought it was more. I do worry that since I already look young, that he will continue to look older faster and the discrepancy will be more noticeable later."

Ann, 28

We are half kidding, but you get the gist: You may want to have a sit-down with Mom and Dad if you witness the following "subtle" behavior:

1. They're setting you up with the neighbor's son, who is barely a freshman in college.
2. They exaggerate the pains of aging, applying arthritis cream liberally while mentioning that this is what you have to look forward to.
3. They reminisce fondly about your ex, who was closer to your age, forgetting that he cheated on you constantly, stole all your money, backed the car over the family dog, and belched the alphabet at Thanksgiving.
4. You mother has ceased all talk of you getting married and having babies and now feels you should "find yourself as a single individual."
5. Your father has adopted the deaf and dumb approach when it comes to your personal life.
6. They attempted to ground you, from their condo in Florida. You live in New York.

7. Your OM may be president of his own company, an Oxford University graduate, a Nobel Prize winner, and have cured cancer, but your parents don't see what the big deal is all about.

8. Your mother "forgets" to invite you to family reunions or holiday dinners because she's afraid you'll bring the OM.

Having your family—from Grandpa to your own kids, if you have them—meet your new boyfriend can be really stressful. Sometimes how your family reacts to your OM, or vice versa, can be a real deal-breaker. Nevertheless, before the big meeting, recognize that your loved ones, big or small, may actually help you become conscious of behaviors or traits (negative or positive) about your older boyfriend that you never picked up on.

🖎 According to Beliza Ann Furman, author of the book *Younger Women-Older Men*, women who are attracted to older men fall into two different categories. They either had a doting father who told them frequently how cute they were and they want a lover who will do the same, or they never had that kind of attention and are desperate for it.

Here's the depiction of an uncomfortable scenario: Your dad isn't talking much, a sure sign he is not impressed, your mom just laughed at his joke (you thank her silently), and then someone starts talking about graduation dates then stops quickly (please, no talk of dates, historical events, or numbers of any sort, you pray silently). You watch yourself vacillate between being your parent's daughter and being your OM's girlfriend as you struggle to maintain your independence in the wake of their disapproval.

Then, depending upon how comfortable you are about making your own decisions and how much you value your parents' opinions, you may have to evaluate how you will be able to live with and withstand their dissent as you hold your ground. After all, you just wanted everyone to get along and see the wonderful things in each other that you two do.

What Are Your Parents Thinking?

If your parents are more on the conservative or traditional side, their thinking probably runs along these lines: Why couldn't she pick someone her age? They are baffled. They question when exactly the psychological trauma occurred, the one they can't figure out, that has lead you into the arms of a man who is closer in age to them than to you. Here are some possible rationalizations from visibly upset parents:

1. You must be rebelling. Or you must secretly be angry at them and want to tick them off. They hope you'll hurry up, grow bored of him, and move on to someone your own age.
2. You have unresolved issues related to your father that has led you to need a man who they think is much more father-like than boyfriend-like. (This of course leads to sniping between them, "You weren't around . . . of course she has issues related to men!" "No, it was you, she obviously picked up on your issues related to your father that you never resolved!")
3. He must be brainwashing you. He has somehow gotten you to put his age aside. Is it with money? His connections and power?
4. You were the little sister at home, so does that mean you are just replaying those dynamics? ("Ugh, this never

would have happened if we'd sent her to volleyball camp like she begged us!")

5. It's obvious he is gaga about her, and she loves being in control. In a relationship with someone her age she'd have to work at being an equal. Well, this is her taking the easy way out with someone she can push around because he's so smitten with her youth!

Meanwhile, all you want is for them to see the great heart this man has, recognize how happy he makes you, and accept the fact that he is not going anywhere any time soon. Is that so hard? The answer could very well be "yes," and you may have to accept the idea that you cannot control what your parents like or value, and that you may have to live your life the way you see fit, without their approval.

In some cases, it is possible that more conservative, traditionally minded parents will become more comfortable with this decision over time. If you have a history of "mistakes" in the relationship department, their skepticism may be well founded until they see longevity in this relationship. Still, others will express their disapproval, either tacitly or explicitly, for as long as they can. But if your parents are less traditional in their values and more open to differences in relationships such as age, they may give you the message that your happiness is more important to them than anything else, and hence, they can be a strong support for you.

How you decide to respond depends on what tends to work with your particular family and its delicate ecology: Do they take a while to assimilate new people/situations? Do they use humor to address important topics? Do they practice avoidance, hoping "the problem" will go away? Above all, if they are skeptical or wary, know that it comes from a good place, keep an open mind, and allow them their opinions.

The OM as a Stepdad

This section is not only just about how he treats your children, it's also about how he works to co-parent with you. Whether you've been a single parent for a while or not, getting used to the presence of your man in the mother-child space can be very challenging indeed. When they play, when they enjoy each other's company, or when he's there to pick up the slack on a rainy day when you have a migraine, these are the times you can really appreciate some older men—especially the older man who has experience with kids.

If he's been there and done that developmental stage before with his own little ones, he may very well be able to give you some valuable guidance. That is, if he knows how to deliver his two cents in a way that doesn't put you on the defensive, and if you're not too sensitive to hear it. Besides, watching him relate to your child is one of the most important ways you can really get to know about your man's values, his people skills, his ability to set limits, and how he conveys tenderness. If you can let an authentic relationship mature without too much orchestrating on your part, you and your child will likely be better off in the long run. If you find yourself meddling, orchestrating, or protecting too much for their relationship to happen organically, you must ask yourself why. If you feel good about their interactions, you may need to learn to take a step back. Alternatively, if there is something that makes you uncomfortable on a gut level, you may need to take a step back from your relation-ship with this man.

Watch and learn, then ask yourself: Is he a . . .

1. **Spoiler:** He lets them get away with it all; gives too much money and candy; turns the other cheek when they're out of line.

2. **Teaser:** Does he believe that he can "toughen them up" with a little adversity, namely practical jokes and teasing?

3. **Buddy:** Does he chase them through the living room during dinner and then look at you expectantly when they're out of control?

4. **Dictator:** Freely impose his "rules" on them without the realization that they are getting used to his presence and may not be the least bit familiar with his way of doing things?

5. **Phantom:** Manages to dart around and in between them? Gently but deftly puts off their requests for attention?

Keep in mind that there is no substitute for a relationship built over time, and it is no different with children. The best and most effective way to exert genuine influence is to build a bond with children based on trust, respect, and compassion. Follow their interpersonal lead; that is to say, when dealing with children, let them establish the pace and move at their own speed. If they are warm and affectionate, he should return in kind; if they are standoffish, he should not take it personally. There simply is no quick fix for this one, but we'll give you some important guidelines to follow when trying to help build his parent platform:

1. Spend quality alone time with your kids. Don't make leisure time include all of you. This helps your children realize that they are not being replaced.

2. Enjoy each other's company very casually and let your child accept him as a friend before introducing the idea of a boyfriend in your life.

3. When you've known each other for a while, let them spend some fun time together without you (e.g., making

cookies together; doing an art project together; or playing sports together).

4. Allow him to stand back from discipline at first and watch how you do things. Gradually he can introduce his authority. Once they are responding to the limits he sets, encourage a gradual increase in setting limits.

5. Do not have open-ended disagreements with him in front of your children unless you can both look at each other, agree to disagree for now, and really move on.

6. When there is friction between them, try to stay objective. Do not automatically stand up for your little one and point the finger at him.

7. Back him up. Explain that you want respectful behavior.

8. Listen to your children if they come to you with repeated complaints, and speak with him about this in private. Do not address the issues in front of everyone involved.

According to James Bray, author of *Stepfamilies*, early on in the relationship, children view stepparents similar to a coach or camp counselor, and even feel that the role of "friend" is ideal. What they need, then, is a relationship in which they can find support and encouragement of positive values. Let's look at some of the issues your (and his) children may be faced with in a new relationship:

1. A new potential stepparent they didn't ask for or choose.
2. Fear of losing contact with either parent.
3. The extinction of the fantasy that Mom and Dad will get back together.

Finally, it is important to try to understand what children are struggling with and the fact that their coping skills are in line with their developmental stages. As a potential stepparent it is important that your older man be able to recognize your child's concerns and not be resentful or take challenging behavior personally. Children need strong support, endless patience, and compassion. While this does not mean that everyday limits are to be suspended, it does mean that keeping their perspectives in mind may help you understand their moods, ideas, and motives and be more patient.

Meet His Family

His family might be very small (depending on whether his parents are still alive) or huge and tangled. Maybe your parents are divorced and remarried; one of his parents might be widowed and has a "friend." Maybe you have an ex-spouse (and perhaps children), and he does as well. Between the two of you it's quite possible that the dynamics of family members and the wide range in ages makes a scenario like that of the Brady Bunch look simple. So who are you to them? The girlfriend who won't last anyway, the second wife, the dreaded "step-monster," or, if he has grown children, you may be the youngest grandmother of all time.

🐍 An article titled "The Second Wives Club" by Carla Rohlfing Leve in the *Ladies' Home Journal* chronicled how hard being a second wife is: "I was in for somewhat of a rude awakening. Although I thought of myself simply as a wife, I quickly learned that the 'second' amendment in front of my title spoke volumes to many people. When I showed off my new ring to my aunt, she told me I had no business marrying a father, strongly implying that I had destroyed another woman's life and contributed to the abandonment of an innocent child. I was shocked that my happy news could be interpreted so falsely. My husband's ex is the one who initiated the divorce. He's a great dad, and my stepdaughter doesn't even hate me. She gives me presents on Mother's Day."

Say the words "second wife," and the image that comes
to mind is a young, inexperienced, home-wrecker who has
no idea what she's in for. Maybe you are just the prospective
second wife. Even the title of "serious girlfriend" can earn
you the grief. Here, then, are the different scenarios you
might encounter with his parents or family, depending on
how traditional or open minded this crowd is:

- Being subtly or overtly compared to his first wife. You
  may be polar opposites or perhaps worse: The two of you
  may be very, very similar.
- Having to cope with his ongoing relationship with his
  first wife as the result of custody arrangements, friends in
  common, or just plain geographical proximity. While an
  amicable relationship between the two of them may help
  ease certain tensions, there is then the possibility that he
  will find it easier to help her out or spend more time with
  her and their children. It may be necessary to "budget"
  the time one, or both of you, spend with your exes.
- Aside from the time-budgeting, there may be, on a purely
  emotional level, the feeling that there are three of you in
  the marriage because her "phantom" is always hovering
  around in pictures or other references.
- And don't forget her response to you. *AARP: The Magazine* published the results of a study titled "The Divorce
  Experience: A Study of Divorce at Midlife and Beyond,"
  which estimated that 66 percent of divorces are initiated
  by women. Given those statistics, her response may range
  from pity (read: you don't know what you are getting
  into, honey) to overt hostility.

How he copes with his parents' or family's behavior can
add fuel to the fire. Does he avoid addressing situations until
the very last moment? Does he escape, duck, and let you

get all the heat? Does he exclude you in an effort to protect you? First and foremost, look to him for clues as to how to deal with his family (as he should do with yours). He might ignore small ripples in conversations because he's found that that works best. If, however, you feel slighted, waiting to bring it up to him until later is best (though hard). Try to solve problems between the two of you rather than place him and his family on the opposing team.

There are very few published rules out there as far as second-wife etiquette goes; however, more guidelines and support are on the horizon. There is, nevertheless, an awful lot of commiserating going on. We Googled "second-wives support" and got 2,030,000 responses which included Second Wives Café (online support for second wives and step-moms), Second Wives Clubs (Sisterhood for Stepmoms), Second Wives Coalition (of the National Family Justice Association), and Steptalk.org.

> **In Her Words**
> "Though Tom was an aggressive businessman, when it came to setting boundaries and rules with his ex-wife, he turned into a spineless wimp! There were times I wanted to grab the phone away from him and scream at her myself."
>
> *Ali, 31*

A Clash of Cultures

The family you grew up in was its own little world, complete with its own culture and values. You can fall head-over-heels in love with your man—older or not—but when it gets around to that time when the two of you start sharing your families by making first introductions, things can get tough. All of a sudden, this wonderful man you fell for has a context, and it's weird or different or just makes no sense to you based on where you come from. If you're wise, you'll find it's a great opportunity to get a firsthand look at how he lived, the interpersonal atmosphere he grew up in, and his response to his family's demands.

"They fight so much. They have these explosive arguments and then the evening just continues as if nobody hurt anybody's feelings and nothing happened. In my family, if you so much as rolled your eyes at my parents you were sent to your room immediately. I'm definitely a confrontation avoider."—Lisa, 24

"My boyfriend's mother was thrilled to meet me: I was someone who was going to take care of her Ted. Their liking me seemed to have so little to do with who I was; it was what I could provide for him."—Keli, 39

"Dan's family was very tight-lipped, and no matter how you really felt, everything was fine. Mine was the opposite: a lot of yelling, affection, and emotions."—Kia, 32

"My OM's father died when he was in college, and his mother was in a nursing home. It was hard to get any information from him about what growing up was like. I finally got to see a photo album and it was like getting a peek into another world. For the most part there was a lot of guessing."—Melissa, 35

"Terrence's parents were both in their eighties, about the age of my grandparents. I felt as if I had inherited a second set of grandparents. It was hard for me not to assume the role of a grandchild, rather than a daughter-in-law. They talked about "the war" as if I knew which one, and were very opinionated about politics and religion. Terrence would humor them and told me to just go along with it."—Jamie, 27

My Family, Myself

Part of the healthy maturation process requires that you examine the origin of your family's beliefs, attitudes, and value systems and take what you want in order to build your own unique values that are consonant with your self-images and self-appraisals. People take the good or what they perceive to be healthy, and let go of what seems to them to be destructive, painful, or obsolete. They make active attempts to break away and consciously recreate themselves as individuals.

Blindly adopting one's family's value system stunts individual growth and hinders the individuation process. You or your boyfriend may genuinely respect and admire numerous facets of your parents' values, or not. The question is, are you open to having this conversation with him? For some, this is a very threatening prospect and tantamount to expulsion from the family. Real fears of abandonment and rejection may arise.

🐾 A survey of 2,631 single people conducted by ItsJustLunch .com found that 42 percent of them wait six months or more before bringing a significant other home.

In a relationship with an older man, it is possible—but not necessarily the case—that he has sorted through these issues over the years. In fact, that just may be one of the things that attracts you so much to him: his ability to separate himself from his parents and their control. Perhaps it gives you hope. If he understands and remembers where in this process he was at your stage of life, he will hopefully have perspective and patience with you. Pressuring each other on this front can be a real source of contention. By the same token, you both need to ask yourselves who exactly you're getting involved with and just how many of you will be in the bed and in the checkbook. The goal is to create your own family with its own unique disposition and values.

Today's Parents Are Hip to It All—Right?

By now, generation after generation has become increasingly comfortable with what were once real hot buttons, such as divorce, homosexuality, surrogate parenting, frozen eggs, sperm banks, and large age differences in couples. There are more controversial problems out there and there's every possibility that parents are more accepting than you might think.

> **In Her Words**
> "We all grow up with the weight of history on us. Our ancestors dwell in the attics of our brains as they do in the spiraling chains of knowledge hidden in every cell of our bodies."
>
> *Shirley Abbott*

When your parents are divorced and your dad is remarried to a woman fifteen years his junior and nine years your senior, chances are he'll be pretty accepting. By the same token, what if your mom is with a man ten years her junior? Depending upon a host of variables including how they grew up and how open-minded they are, they will or will not be supportive. Some parents are critical no matter what, and if it wasn't his age, it'd be his shoe size. Remember one thing: If you value your OM's perspective he may prompt you to be more open-minded and look at things from all sides. He may tell you not to be too quick to dismiss their ideas just because they're your parents.

Rules of Conduct for Meeting His Parents/Family or His Meeting Yours

- Bring a small gift or at least the typical small bouquet of flowers.
- Don't start using first names unless the parents formally ask you to.
- Don't ever talk about sex in front of your families.
- Don't ask if they mind if you two go ahead and share a bed at their house.
- If offered a drink, accept. If it's alcohol, drink moderately.
- Don't smoke unless they are smoking.
- Even if you're not hungry or thirsty, don't refuse food or drink.
- Do show humor but only appropriate humor.
- Do give some thought to the answers you'll be giving to questions they'll most likely ask you (e.g., where you grew up, jobs you have held, and so on).
- And, of course, avoid swear words or cursing.

One surefire tip when meeting his family for the first time? Tell stories that highlight the wonderful qualities of their son. All parents, regardless of their son's age, like hearing how resourceful, kind, and creative their children are.

From Their Perspective: What Parents Think

During one interview of women aged twenty-six to fifty-two, we discussed the dilemma of really disliking your twenty-something daughter's boyfriend. Two camps with fierce opinions basically emerged. The younger, single women and some of the married women with no children strongly expressed the opinion that a twenty-something is old enough to choose her own boyfriends and understandably doesn't want her mother interfering in her love-life. The mothers, on the other hand, made a passionate argument that their twenty-something daughter, even if responsible and intelligent, had not yet developed the kind of perspective on life and men that would prompt her to extricate herself from a "bad" situation. As mothers who considered their offspring the heaviest of investments, they felt compelled to play a hand in "surrounding" their eligible daughters with the "right" kind of guys.

"My daughter Lisa finally introduced us to her boyfriend of six months. She had warned us he was older than she but hadn't given us specifics. I couldn't guess his age by his looks. It might be two years, it might be eight, I thought. I liked him. Only much afterward did she tell us he was fifteen years older! He was seven years younger than I was! I thought I would be more open-minded but caught myself wishing she had picked someone closer to her in age."—Loretta

"I thought Kendra and Tom looked ridiculous together; it embarrassed me to be around them in public. He was so obviously older than she was that she looked like a little girl next to him. I wondered if people could figure out who was related to whom at our dinner table. My Kendra was so beautiful that she could have had any young man from college that she wanted, but now she had the burden of a divorced man who'd be old and frail when she was still young. I cringed seeing them hold hands." —Rochelle

"I tried hard not to think about this man who was closer to my age than hers being her boyfriend. It was almost hard to look at him in the eyes. At times I felt like telling him I needed a moment alone with him, then asking him what the hell he was doing. He did, however, seem very respectful of her. He treated her like an equal and she seemed calm and happy. I guess that is what is important."—David

In a "Dear Doctor" question Dr. Belisa Vranich got when writing for the *New York Daily News*, a reader asked how much it mattered if you got along with your prospective in-laws. Dr. Belisa answered that there were two factors to consider: how geographically close they were and how emotionally enmeshed they were. If you get a very for the first and highly for the second, brace yourself for trouble.

Hopefully meeting your prospective in-laws will go smoothly. Be patient with them, and be patient with yourself. It's a big step!

five

His Kids: Like Cute Little Thorns in Your Side

Let's not sugarcoat it. There is every possibility that his kids—whether eight years old or thirty-eight years old—will have a fierce dislike for you, without even knowing you one bit! It may feel like prejudice, but from their point of view, you may have stepped into their mom's old role or you may be far too young to be dating him for sincere purposes. There is a fine balance here between understanding where they are coming from and letting them take advantage of a situation in the name of painful feelings. They have every right to their feelings, but not every right to certain behaviors. Depending upon their age and the dynamic between them and their parents, you can win them over, but it can be a tough climb. Some things you might want to remember:

- Kids, in general, have an instinct, the ability to sniff out our weaknesses and find our buttons—whether you have kids of your own or you've never even changed a diaper.
- Kids will test you in ways you've never been called out before, and when you're viewed as Mommy's rival or replacement, watch out.

- If they're old enough to understand that their dad is dating someone, they're old enough to realize how much younger than their mother you may be. Perhaps they've also noticed that their father is happier than he's ever been, happier than when he was married to their mother and all were still living under the same roof.
- On a more purely emotional level, kids of any age may perceive and react to you as another sibling vying for and taking away Dad's attention and affection.
- Withdrawn or aggressive behavior toward you may have, at its roots, sadness and anger toward him for leaving in the first place.
- Keep in mind that adult children—even those similar in age to you—may have reactions that are "childlike."
- Adult children may be nonchalant and surprise you with their sincere and genuine welcome.
- Many of the same rules you use with his adolescent children or his friends—taking it slow and not trying too hard—apply when dealing with adult children.

ᔑ Researchers say that most families take from one to three years to adjust to a divorce. Some families can take five years or longer, depending on the situation surrounding the divorce.

So can you get past these obstacles? There is no guarantee. Sometimes it's downright tricky, but if you know your heart is in the right place, don't beat yourself up and definitely don't give up.

Rules for Dealing with His Kids

Let's start out with five simple rules that will prepare the ground for a longer, stable relationship:

1. Don't just plunk yourself down and start giving orders.
2. By the same token, don't try to be their new best friend.
3. Don't try and trick them into thinking you're "cool" by using their language and their electronic toys.
4. If they're close to or in their teens, adding them as a friend to your MySpace page, for example, is a bad, bad idea.
5. Do not move in too quickly. They may be sick and tired of women trying to form an instant bond with them in an invasive or disingenuous way, or maybe they're not yet used to girlfriends coming in and out of his life.

Authenticity is the key here. Be true to who you are and treat them with respect. Your best bet is to maintain a safe distance (we'll define this as not sleeping over while they're around; not insisting they "play" with you; and not showing a lot of physical affection with Dad in front of them) until your relationship with their father becomes more serious. That way, when the time comes to actually deal with the presence of his children, you do not have to undo any damage caused early on. Give them the chance to warm up to you from a distance.

Just remember the basics. You're not automatically the mother. At first, you're the babysitter they torture or the substitute teacher whose limits they test to the nth degree. What you may not realize, however, is that your relative youth and energy can make you easy to relate to as well as a great playmate for the younger ones, and interacting with you can be a more nonthreatening one-on-one experience. As a lead-in, this can be a great way to build a real relationship. Acknowledge that you're not Mommy, and you'll never be Mommy. Never, never openly bad-mouth Mommy. It's bad for the kids and will make them suffer; it's bad for your image, and can be bad, bad, bad for the relationship.

🐾 A large number of divorces occur in families with children under the age of eighteen. Parental conflict can hinder children's adjustment, and good co-parenting skills are very important to a child's adjustment. A quarter of children whose parents divorce experience ongoing emotional and behavioral difficulties (as compared to 10 percent of children whose parents do not divorce).

Take it slow. Remember—they didn't pick you, Daddy did. You've been foisted upon them. Give them space and let them come to you. This means on macro and micro levels. In other words, say "hello," and begin a conversation, but if you don't get much in return, let it go. Don't try harder. Just greet them and then let them start the conversation. Then follow their lead; don't try to engineer a conversation you think they'll really like. Take the same approach with play or fun activities. Suggestions are okay, but follow their lead more often and it will be a more meaningful experience to them.

If You're Not a Mother

Whether it's book- or street-smarts, you're smart, you're mature, you're hard-working, and if you're single you're independent . . . and then, suddenly, you're the babysitter! "Wait just a minute!" you're thinking, as you stroll into Starbucks with his elementary school–aged offspring who may very well be behaving like little banshees, "How exactly did I get here?" Not only did it seem like a good idea when he brought up the possibility of you "taking the kids for a while," it was downright flattering. Heck, you've been charged with the utmost responsibility. Being the caretaker of his kids really pulls you into his life, his reality. And if you love this man and truly believe that you want a future with him, you'd better make peace with that reality *now* because those little (or maybe big) ones are there for the whole ride. Besides, you are in fact an adult with the potential of making a lifelong impact on their little psyches. So whether you marry him or not, you are the maker of a potentially lasting impression on these children.

If You Are a Mother

As you already know, being a mother can make you feel eminently more comfortable with children in general, especially those in the same age categories as your own. That's no guarantee however, that it'll be easy to connect with his children. Today's blended families are nothing like the *Brady Bunch* paradise we saw in the 1970s. Those kids accepted Mike and Carol at face value and there was never a single episode in which anyone felt any of the growing pains that come along with being in a real-life blended family.

For starters, there are the same issues as above in terms of developing an authentic relationship with them at an appropriate pace, but you already have a discipline and childrearing philosophy that you've put into effect with your own kids. In a dream scenario, you and your man learn from each other and are willing to take advice or get a more objective "outsider" perspective, while in the worst-case scenario, you wind up like two opposing football teams poised and ready to take each other down. You need to try your best to be sensitive to each other and understand that both of you may feel like you're walking on eggshells around the other's children. Your relationship with your natural children is well, natural. In fact, research shows that men especially have a much stronger desire to provide and care for their biological offspring. Thankfully, though, we are a malleable species when it comes to loving our children—just look at the strong and healthy ties that can be the outcome of adoption. And there's even the possibility, if you're both open to it, that you can learn and become better parents in the process of blending.

Attack of the Step-Monster

The word stepmother often has a mean connotation. Mean and evil stepmothers, ones that monopolize Father's attention and manage to negotiate an allowance cut, often come to mind. The fairy-tale scenario has the father widowed and blind to this woman's mission to control the family. While there is no word for soon-to-be stepmother, "girlfriend" is what is usually used. Title aside, you may very well have already jumped into the stepmother role without even trying. What drives the little ones to use the dreaded "step-monster" term when referring to you? It may be something you are doing that you can work on and change, or it may be something the child brings to your relationship from his or her emotional makeup that you have less control over.

"My dad's girlfriend tries to be our mom. She isn't and will never be."—Charlie, 9

"She is prettier than my mom. He pays more attention to her and I know my mom feels sad about it. It makes me feel bad for my mom."—Rachel, 13

"She was really nice in the beginning, but now she tries to make rules. She changed."—Kenny, 7
"Dad used to spend time just with us. Now it's always the three of us. I liked it better before."—Dierdre, 11
Some of men we interviewed did not see the more subtle nuances around the difficulty of being a stepmother or new

family member. Often the hostility comes from the female members of the family: sisters and cousins. In *Forced to Be Family: A Guide for Living with Sinister Sisters, Drama Mamas, and Infuriating In-Laws,* author Cherly Dellasega writes:

> Biological or social sisterhood can be intensely supportive or devastatingly destructive. . . . While the type of bond may vary, the behaviors are strikingly similar: exclusion, ridicule, gossip, and a host of other relationally aggressive behaviors that fan the flames of "kitchen wars." These emotional battles among female relatives are larger in magnitude and impact than the offenses of even dearest friends. More love, more difficulty, more anguish, and more of everything are the hallmarks of both distant and close female relationships within families. Although the vow "for better or worse" is voluntary in marriage, we don't have a choice about the women we grow up with or those who enter our families and our lives for decades when we're adults.

According to a 2004 survey reported in *AARP: The Magazine,* 42 percent of the men said that their worst fears after the divorce involved their children, with most of these men worrying they'd lose contact with their kids. In comparison, only 15 percent of women had these fears.

The stepfamily will be the family of the future. Today, one of every four children is a stepchild. The two most prevalent myths are the character of "evil stepmother" and the concept of instant love. Nancy K. Recker of Ohio State University writes that:

> There are over 900 stories written about evil or wicked stepmothers. They are particularly common in fairy tales, which suggest that stepmothers are comparable to wild animals and supernatural beings that treat children wickedly. In the past,

the stepmother's role was to replace the child's biological mother who had died. Many of these bad examples are seen in such stories as *Cinderella* and *Snow White* where children are portrayed as victims who hate their stepmothers. On the opposite front is the myth that love between family members will happen immediately. As the nun-turned-governess-turned-wife in the Rodgers and Hammerstein musical about the von Trapp family, Maria brims with emotional sincerity and childlike joy.

As one would expect in a musical from the 1950s, the von Trapp kids in *The Sound of Music* fall in love with her instantly. Real life is not written by Rogers and Hammerstein, and blending a family takes work, time, and patience.

Coping with Your New Role and Coping with His Children

Here's how to handle them, one age group and one situation at a time, so you know you've done your very best to build an authentic, caring, and positive connection with them.

The Younger Set: Early Childhood Through Elementary School

They may have an easier time with a new parent figure in their lives because they are at an age where family involvement is at the core of their emotional needs. This may make them more open to forming a parent/child relationship with you, especially if you can create a genuine connection with them. One word of caution however: This age group can also feel the pangs of competition and jealousy more intensely, and so they feel more threatened.

When they're young and sweet, there is the possibility of the instant love connection. What a way to start! They're little and cute and frequently compliant and obviously vulnerable. Whether you have experience with kids or not, whether you like them or not, these are the easiest to bond with. They'll take your help, they'll take your direction, and they'll likely look up to you with adoration and admiration. The parents of these little ones are doing some basic things very right. This is the child who has a history (however short) of loving and supportive care, and reasonable limits that have been skillfully set. They've been well primed for additional healthy relationships with adults who can handle them. Have fun with them. Let yourself laugh and enjoy the time you spend with them. When you are with them, let them take the lead in play and follow along. They will absolutely *love* it. Listen to what they volunteer, as opposed to interviewing them about what you think matters to them. You will get to know them, and they you, in an authentic way. Don't be surprised if even these little ones push the occasional limit, they all do at times. And don't be afraid to set limits with them. All kids need limits.

When they're young and not so sweet, shrouded in challenging, provocative behavior, the love connection is still a very reachable goal. After all, little ones are not quite as hardened and a bit more accessible emotionally. You can do this. If you're in the company of a "not-so-sweet" little one, you need to step back and remind yourself that this is a young child. He or she is bringing their style of relating to adults at large into their relationship with you, and isn't conscious of it. Translation: They are going to have the same behaviors, expectations, and habits with you as they do with any female authority figure. Don't take it personally!

Provocative behaviors in this age group can range from blatant defiance, ("Put your seatbelt on," "*No!*") to the good old public temper tantrum. Provided that you have permission (implicit or explicit) to step in when needed, do so. There are two critical things to remember here: (1) an ounce of cure is worth a pound of prevention; that is, build a really nice, authentic connection with them, give them lots of praise when they deserve it, and then they will be much more likely to respond when you must exact a limit; and (2) be firm but stay cool, cool, cool. Losing your temper with them gives them implicit permission to lose theirs.

LITTLE GIRLS

They just want to copy everything you do, so set a good example. They can be like little sponges, taking in your every move. They're watching what you wear, how you put on your makeup, the way you walk and talk, and how you tend to their needs. Now watch them when they're playing family. Your role will be in there and you will get to see yourself in action as they imitate you down to the inflection in your voice. Expect to be asked to engage in symbolic play (e.g., "Let's play school and I'll be the teacher"); to play with dolls; to cook; and to do art projects. Not that lots of little girls don't enjoy sports or playing in dirt, but these scenarios are not as typical.

LITTLE BOYS

Put on your gym clothes and sneakers. You *will* be running around, quite possibly in the mud. Again, while lots of little boys enjoy dolls and art projects, we want to help you plan for the more common scenario. It usually involves taking one object and bashing another while shouting "arghh, arghh" just to see what will happen to the bashed object or to cultivate feelings of physical strength and physical mastery. Throwing balls, chasing, scaring with pretend monsters, making mud, and digging up bugs are all delicacies on the "little boy play in the park" menu. So, as we mentioned earlier, don't wear your Manolo Blahniks. Do wear your Nikes and expect to be shooting hoops, catching, dodging, and throwing stuff. While you can leave the wrestling for Dad, little boys will really appreciate an active playmate when you're playing together in the park. At home, there are often the same themes on a smaller scale; that is, they happen between little army men or other little figurines. But the bottom line should be *no* running, chasing, scaring, and so on in the house.

The Elementary-Schooler

While some of the same gender stereotypes exist, these kids are no longer as emotionally up-front as their younger counterparts. These guys are sussing you out with a higher level of sophistication, and deciding what they do or don't like about you on the basis of how they've been treated, what they've been taught to value, and how much you remind them of either the "so mean" or the "really nice" teacher.

Academic success and the discipline it takes to get homework done are major focal points of their lives. Their self-esteem is typically wound up with their success or lack thereof at school activities, be they in the books or on the field. Don't dole out unwarranted compliments. Give them real feedback about their accomplishments, politely of course, (e.g., "It looks like you really gave it your all" versus "That is the *best* in the class," or "Your hard work shows, keep it up and you'll get to the top" versus "You're the *best* player on the whole team"). Don't insist they are the best reader in the class or the best T-ball player on the field when you know they're not, because they know they're not and they know you know they're not! Their challenging behaviors are often subtler and can be aimed at something "about" you rather than just the generic tantrum or defiant "No!" More often you'll encounter storming off in a huff, lying about homework or other responsibilities, passive-aggressive jabs at siblings or you, martyrdom in the form of dramatic declarations about how "unfair" it all is, or how they "never" get the stuff they want, and so on. Rules and fairness are paramount in their minds so they are constantly getting hung up on perceived inequities. "He got to stay up later," "She got a bigger cookie," "I didn't lose, no fair—you cheated!"

As mentioned before, keep cool and build a positive relationship from the get-go. This is some of the best insurance during rocky times. But when you do have to set a limit, remember selective ignoring and praising (more on this in the discipline section).

Pre-Teens and Young Adolescents (Eleven to Fourteen)

This age group is probably the most challenging. The combination of their newfound critical thinking skills, improved arguing ability, and increased desire for independence mixed in with a perspective that is still rooted in childhood fantasy, makes them very strong willed and oppositional at times. It is especially important with this age group to bond first and discipline later.

Then there's the Dreaded Middle-Schooler. Just face the facts. If they're not idolizing you—there's no way out of it—yes, yes, and yes, they are laughing at you: at what you wear, how you speak, what your eyebrows look like, how you chew—heck, how you inhale. It's not as juvenile as the elementary-aged kid and not as controlled as the high schooler who is trying much harder to be an adult. In short, it's honed yet not harnessed and can be some pretty vicious stuff. "Your nose looks like a potato in that hat." "Don't you ever wash that jacket? You wear it like every day." Here's when you can start to experience rejection from a hardened creature who seems impossible to break for long enough to say a genuine "hello," never mind bond with.

Don't let it dampen the sparks with your man by either dwelling on it and moaning about this, that, or the other comment you should've and could've made. Do watch how Daddy negotiates these sharp little jabs. Does he ignore or explode? Hopefully it's somewhere in between. If it's one of these extremes, you can still follow your own path. Whether he's paying way too much attention to bad behavior by giving lecture after lecture (which only winds up reinforcing) or trying to avoid it until he just can't take it anymore and then exploding, you can work on ignoring what's rude, reinforcing what's nice with smiles and verbal praise, and standing your own ground when pressured with manipulative or rude behaviors. Remember, though, you may have to endure some adolescent anger aimed right at you. If you can, you may very well have to draw a line in the sand that they realize they can't cross. They'll have more respect for you in the long run.

Teens and Young Adults
(Ages Fifteen and Up)

This group is busy breaking away from and in the process of forming their own identities outside of the family. Consequently, they are probably less involved in the blended family and need less active parenting as well. That is not to imply that they do not need to have limits set for them. As with the pre-teen group, it is very important to bond before attempting to discipline.

High-schoolers and the college-bound are in an altogether different scenario. In fact, your age may force you into a strange category for them: the half-generation older girl/woman who's not really young enough to be a peer, but not old enough to be seen in an authoritative position either. It is important that you are sensitive to their emergent sexuality and the fact that they may feel very uncomfortable with public displays of affection.

While this age group can be particularly challenging, as you don't have the authoritative role to fall back on, they can also be a real pleasure. Talk to them about just about anything. If you listen with an open and nonjudgmental mind, you stand the chance of forming a real bond with them.

Hang out and enjoy the overlaps in your generations' pop culture but don't get too cozy by forgetting your age and position and laughing or bonding over something inappropriate, like something you know their father forbids. For example, don't make fun of the algebra tutor, dismiss pot smoking as no big deal, or even share a laugh about the way Dad chews. Before you know it, you'll be invited on a double date with his daughter and her boyfriend's cousin.

By the same token, don't fall back on an air of superiority in an attempt to separate yourself from them. It will most likely come across as hollow and ineffective. You'll get laughed at and then promptly chewed up and spit out. Sure you may run across the shy, more reserved teen, but watch out for the passive-aggressive, or just plain aggressive, bombshells. Like sucker punches, they'll come flying at you when you least expect them, and seem connected to no apparent event. It might take you a day or two to make the connection but when you make it, it'll smart at least as much as the one you actually saw coming. Case in point, the teen who feigns illness or some other "emergency" to make Dad late for your night out at the theater or your special dinner reservations.

Be middle of the road here. After you have held back and waited to form somewhat of a bond, or some familiarity at least, you can let them know that you understand their particular dilemma (can't stay out past curfew, can't have boyfriend over with closed bedroom door, can't go to college parties when they're young teenagers, and so on). When you're being appealed to in an attempt to get what they want, let them know that your hands are tied in the limit-setting department and that it's up to their mom and dad. If they come to you with stories of seeming unreasonable parental behavior, again try and stay neutral, but do talk to them about your experiences and the value of making the best possible choice. Be realistic when talking about possible consequences.

Don't be afraid to discuss anything with them, but always let them know up front that it's their parents, not you, who make the big decisions. And finally, do *not* share with them the one (or two) times you just tried (insert illegal substance here) once. You got away with it; they may not.

What to Do in the Beginning Stages

So how do you do it? Bottom line: You're not their mother, not even close, and you're not their friend. So how are you to interact with them and how are they to interact with this person who doesn't quite fit into their lives, yet has seemingly taken over? Number one piece of advice: Do not attempt a takeover, even if you see absurdities, inequities, and examples of getting away with murder flying all over the place between them and their parents. Remember, they've limped along without you for a long time and no one is less welcome than a "system changer," never mind a system changer who's also Dad's girlfriend. That is, an outsider who comes along and disrupts their happy little homeostatic system.

Dysfunctional as it may be, it's theirs and you have to find your place gradually. If it doesn't make sense to you or, worse, seems destructive, find your place without compromising your own beliefs, but don't be the bull in a china shop who lectures, critiques, or accuses.

Whether Daddy is spoiling or over punishing, if it feels wrong, don't comment or try to take over on the spot. Wait for a time when you're alone together and you've given thought to what you want to say.

You do need to do some groundwork by gathering information. Sit back and be a good observer, but don't be afraid to ask direct questions (e.g., "I really want to develop a nice relationship with Sarah, so how can I be a good partner to you when we're all together?" or "How do you handle the toughest times with Ethan?" or "When Emily's not listening, how can I be helpful?"). After you've inquired, it's critical that you listen, *really listen*, to what he says. His response will fall somewhere on the continuum of "Go ahead and do what you think is best" to "Do it my way here." If he is not the most verbal or direct person, you can also pick up on what is important to him by watching how he responds in actual situations with his kids. Look at all the nonverbal elements of his communication in his facial expressions, body language, and tone of voice. Does he convey happiness and contentment or does he look uptight, nervous, or frustrated? Is any of it directed at you? This early step is also a great way to get to know the man you're with. After all, we can all present our values and belief systems on a silver platter over a cozy dinner in a great restaurant, but nothing is as revealing as the answers we get from direct questions or from watching our partners in action with their little ones.

After you've made your observations and listened to his answers, it's important to think about them on your own. Does what he says make intuitive sense to you? Does it sound overly punitive or too lax? How does it relate to your own childhood and what felt good or bad? How does the scene look? Is he relating to his kids? Are they out of control or behaving like little automatons?

Whether dealing with kids is new to you or not, it can be really helpful at this point to talk with friends or family members who have more experience with kids. The bottom line here is, if something feels or looks *really* bad, take a giant step back. This is part of your man's style of relating and, if it hasn't shown itself in your relationship yet, it will probably be a part of the dynamic you two share. That's not to say you have to agree on everything, or that everything has to feel perfectly wonderful to you.

> ♪ Since he's older, if he has kids, chances are they'll be closer to your age as well. Whether this causes more competition or camaraderie can't be foretold, however here are three things you should not be tempted to say:
>
> *I'm here, get used to it.* (No way; they *are the ones who are here*. You *are only his girlfriend*.)
>
> *This is great; it's like we're sisters.* (Oh really? Can I borrow your Gucci stilettos for the prom? *Yeah, I didn't think so*.)
>
> *I understand what you're going through.* (No, you really don't.)

Once you have an idea of what you like, what makes sense to you, what seems to be contradictory, or absurd even, and what makes you feel less than comfortable, then it's time to act, keeping in mind his wishes of course. When you're on the same page, you can be great partners and really enjoy your time together with him and his kids, as well as expand your role to take on some of the guidance and discipline. By the same token, when the two of you are not on the same page it's time to get in the game. You might give some sort of verbal indicator that you are ready to take on more of a parenting role during your times together ("I know I'm not his mother, but I'm here with you guys a lot and I really care about Jake. When things are tough, mind if I help?" or "Can I give you my perspective on the way things are going?"), or you might feel that the time is right to just jump in. Either way, when he has kids, your relationship has an additional dimension. And how he parents also says a lot about how he relates to others, especially you.

Finally, and perhaps most importantly: Make sure you have a good partner. Is he supportive? Does he listen to your concerns and respect your feelings? Make sure you do the same for him, and you stand the best chance of compromising and working together as an effective team that, by the way, is a tremendous gift for his kids. To be exposed to two adults in a loving, caring relationship, who are able to compromise and work together, teaches children about how healthy relationships work. Whether you marry this man or not, feel very good about making this contribution while you're together. It may have a profound impact on the lives of his children—whether they are two years old or twenty— and their later relationships.

Drawing Lines in the Sand

This section can help you cope once you are at the point in your relationship where you've bonded and you're part of the limit-setting process. Since this is not a book about discipline itself, we'd like to arm you with the very basics, which can be quite effective. The first and best part of any discipline plan here is to remember that old adage, "An ounce of prevention is worth a pound of cure," which means that the best outcomes of limit-setting happen when a good relationship has already been established. Also, always think to yourself about why defiant or difficult behavior is happening. Remember, these are kids who are probably not ready or able to articulate all that they feel. You may want to manip-ulate something in the environment before you embark on disciplining a child. As a ten-year-old boy once said to his therapist: "As soon as I get used to the rules and everything at my mom's, it's time to change again and go to my dad's!" He tended to sulk and, if pressed, become completely defi-ant. His mother and father learned to give him lots of space when he first arrived. He was allowed to go and play for a while without talking or answering questions. This gave him time to decompress and he was then much more ame-nable to accepting limits.

Another example of changing things in the environ-ment before attempting to set a limit here would be to try and establish a welcoming routine that is easy and happens around something that feels good to the child. If time per-mits, go and get a snack together at their favorite place or try and have comforting things out at home when they arrive. Another common emotional under layer of difficult behav-ior is that there may be some resentment relating to the cus-tody arrangement. They live with their mother and see their father only now and then while you have him mostly to yourself. Make sure not to take this personally and remem-ber to give your man some time alone with his kids without feeling left out or making him feel guilty.

Handling Defiance and Difficult Behavior

Believe it or not, the number one most important strategy here is praise. Yes, whenever you see it (and you should be making efforts to find it if it's not too obvious), praise good behavior. This includes good manners, sharing toys, waiting patiently to take turns, cheering on a friend, compromising when they don't get their way, and obeying when you can tell they really don't want to. Praise with comments, smiles, and hugs (when you're close enough). Second tactic: Ignore behavior you don't want to see more of. This includes whining, sulking, and tenacious attempts to wear you down to get what they want ("Please, please. I promise I'll be good for the rest of my life and never ask you for anything again!" or "But why? Why? Why not? Just tell me why. Just tell me!"). Ignore means just *that*, ignore. No eye contact, no response, and *no* lectures. If the "wear you down" behavior becomes too persistent or aggressive, however, do respond. Let the offender know that if they persist, there will be consequences.

The final tactic is explaining logical and natural consequences. You should have them on hand, meaning you and their father need to have a planning meeting about this one beforehand. That's right, sit down and come up with a list of what you think are fair consequences. The golden rule of thumb here is not to over punish. Don't take toys or privileges away for a week. For little ones, take them for five to ten minutes per year of age. For older kids, you can take them away for an afternoon or a day. Use time-outs as a way to take away the privilege of being in a social situation and to help them calm down. These are examples of logical consequences. Natural consequences happen when you don't intervene and the environment bestows something less than pleasurable. For example, don't try and help the seventh grader convince the teacher to extend the due date on his report. If he goofed off, don't be afraid to let him fail.

When Things Are Getting to You

You may notice relationship patterns between the kids and their dad that bug you, but remember one thing: Try, try, try not to let it push your buttons. Watching a particular scene may subconsciously send you back to the dynamic in your own home when you were this particular age and relating to your father (or even your mom). As Socrates said, "Know thyself." And when you do, you can be aware of your personal button pushers in any heated situation, not just this one, and you can navigate out of trouble by knowing how to make the distinction between your past and the present reality. You are twenty-, thirty-, or even forty-something now, you have better coping skills, and you are more aware of your own dad as an imperfect person with his own baggage. What's happening here now in this mall may look a lot like what you went through and you can even relate to his kid, but in the year 2008, you have a new and more objective perspective on this situation. Your man is not the villain here just because his response may be similar to what you recall getting from your dad. By the same token, his kid is not a villain just because he's using a manipulative or frustrating coping mechanism.

There may be lots of similarities and it may be frustrating, annoying, or even upsetting. The smartest thing to do here is often to wait. Wait and think about your approach instead of blurting out an emotionally charged remark that you may later really regret. Doing this can disrupt your relationship with the kids and with your man as well. Here are some relationship styles or patterns you may notice, and how to deal with the troublesome behavior when you're alone with the kids.

- **Tantrums:** These appear when the kids are used to Dad giving in out of guilt or the desire to avoid a crying, whining fit. This one is simple: Endure the fit. As long as they're not hurting themselves or anyone else, let them cry it out.
- **Bulldozing:** This happens when the kiddies defiantly push right on over a poorly set limit. Ignore the threats,

they are just provocation. When and if they do defy you, however, stay cool and whip out one of those pre-made consequences. Give no more than a couple of warnings and then follow through.

- **Negotiating:** They use this tactic when they're used to wearing Daddy down. Another simple one: Stop talking to them. How can they negotiate when they have no one to negotiate with?

- **The Adult Kid:** Who's who? This is the case when the child is under the false impression that he/she is the adult, and they speak to you using adult terms and with very adult tones of voice. Really the most effective tactic here is to ignore and then respond with happiness and/or praise when they do use a more appropriate tone of voice.

- **Button Pushers:** They'll say you're weak, you're a bad parent, you made Daddy leave Mommy, you know you can't deal with me, get me this now!

- **Lightning Rods:** They inject themselves in the middle, taking the heat from the two in the argument. Protect these kids by defining roles and giving reassurance.

- **Love Sponges:** They are constantly looking for attention and affection, the operative word here being "constantly." Whatever the underlying cause, this behavior has been reinforced by giving all the attention they're craving. Selective ignoring is a key strategy here. Ignore when what you get the feeling that they're looking for excess attention, but do give praise and attention when it's truly warranted.

Ironically, the hardest people to win over may be those walking around with half his genes—even if they have the same silly snort or terrible parallel parking skills. Take your time finding your place in his family, knowing there will be a range of good, bad, subtle and not-too-subtle reactions.

Above all, keep good communication open between the two of you—you may need each other for support, and certainly for the celebrations.

six

Self, Identity, and Assertive Behavior: The Building Blocks of Healthy Relationships

This chapter examines the concept of *self*. While there are many definitions used in classic psychology, a good definition for our purposes is, "a sense of our unique existence among others."

This sense of uniqueness may be considered the foundation of one's personal identity. *Identity*, then, is a person's essential, continuous self; the internal, subjective concept of oneself as an individual. When examining the self and one's identity, the key words to keep in mind are "unique," "continuous" and "essential." The sense of self and identity accompany people everywhere, especially when they walk into any relationship, romantic or not. This sense of self is subject to influence or change depending on how well developed and solid it is, and, of course, the health of the relationship.

Rubberband Boundaries

Another basic psychology term to keep in mind while reading this chapter is "ego boundary," which, for the sake of ease, we will refer to as "boundary." Boundaries are the forces that separate people and make them distinct. Imagine the "self" as a round circle, encased in a ring, which we call the "boundary." Boundaries are more like rubber bands, and their stretch indicates what you can tolerate in a relationship or how much leeway you are willing to give your significant with respect to what bothers, frightens, hurts, or angers you. It is the interplay between the "self" circle and the rubber band "boundary" that creates an identity. Weak boundaries may lead to a rapid alignment of the ideas or values of another person at the expense of one's own identity. Thus, a person's sense of self and identity is maintained or preserved by appropriately strong boundaries.

Strong boundaries should not be rigid; they should allow some flexibility as the loved one's way of doing things is taken into account. Strong boundaries help a person accommodate loved ones' needs and expectations and see their points of view, yet enable an individual to maintain his or her established sense of self and identity in the face of a frightening reality such as separation from, or loss of, a loved one.

Defending Your Turf

A simple illustration could be the internal anxiety generated within when a girlfriend openly disagrees with her boyfriend about the way his mother treats her. This is an attempt to preserve her own unique beliefs or value system while dealing with a very sensitive issue. In the face of this, the boyfriend may leave in an angry huff, perhaps putting out the implicit message that he will leave her. Depending upon how much anxiety this causes her, she may keep quiet next time, or even act in ways that espouse his beliefs in order to appease him, thereby preserving the status quo of the relationship and avoiding future suffering in the form of fear of abandonment.

Calmly, clearly, and firmly delineating boundaries and limits is often what psychologists refer to as "assertive behavior." Being assertive is when you can express yourself in a calm, objective manner in a situation where emotion could easily get the upper hand. It is when you neither blow your stack in an impulsive fit of anger nor sit in the corner like a wallflower, afraid to express yourself. The very idea of being assertive may seem frightening or threatening, as in the illustration above, but once mastered, can be very liberating and comforting. Having early support during childhood means growing up in a loving, supportive, and safe environment, in which the inevitable conflict between parents and siblings was handled with maturity. In sum, assertive behavior was modeled by parents. This early support and modeling of assertion lays the foundation (the building blocks) for both the courage and skill needed to communicate in the context of an intimate relationship in ways that truly express what you believe and what you value without experiencing an overwhelming fear of loss.

Successful assertion of your limits or boundaries early on in a relationship may help weed out the guys who are going to push you beyond your tolerance level with some of their behaviors. It will ultimately lead to finding a better match with a man who recognizes and respects your limits, even if he does not agree with them. The healthy relationship requires that you, too, learn to respect his limits, even when you disagree. In this way, there is the existence and preservation of two separate identities. A healthy relationship requires understanding that you can be very different as individuals and still be close as a couple, that love is not "sameness," that true intimacy demands that you try to be as clear as you can about who you are with yourself and with others.

The Authentic You

This is not to give the impression that women should be emotional superiors who couldn't care less about what others think. People all need other people, they all react to how they are treated, and they all care to different degrees about others' perceptions. It is to what degree that speaks to the integrity and strength of the knowledge and acceptance of the self. A whole self is a mix of the ability to be vulnerable and the ability to be strong. An authentic self is not a hollow representation of who you think your boyfriend wants you to be in order for you to feel loved and accepted by him.

The false belief that a woman can "save" her boyfriend or loved ones, or that she must be their ultimate "caretaker" is an example of neglecting or abandoning oneself and operating only on someone else's behalf. This kind of self-sacrifice, in which you forfeit your identity in the name of "helping," is unhealthy for all. The beneficiaries of your "help" can become passive, dependent people who forfeit their identities in a tradeoff to avoid facing the pain of having to grow up and become functioning adults. As there is danger in abandoning yourself by operating only on the behalf of others, there is also danger in operating only on your own behalf. This failure to recognize others as distinct individuals often shows itself as an insistence that others think, feel, and act as you believe they should.

Early Love

Finally, a word on the development of the self in childhood and how this impacts behavior and perceptions in love relationships. According to a study done by Janice Kennedy in 1999, family functioning and attachment style to parents during early childhood has a significant effect on the quality of attachment to romantic partners in adulthood. Her study showed that adults who reported the healthiest type of "secure" attachment to romantic partners also came from families that were characterized by expressiveness, closeness, valuing independence, and giving encouragement to grow. Essentially, mental health begets mental health: Secure attachments in childhood help develop the ability to form secure attachment to romantic partners as adults.

> ✍ Developmental research has consistently found that a secure infant attachment to a primary caregiver has predicted inter- and intrapersonal competence and well-being later on.

Now that we've spoken about the basic psychological building blocks of a healthy relationship, let's problem solve with real-life examples you can relate to and changes you can perhaps implement if needs be.

Acts of Self-Preservation

The following scenarios depict women in older-man/younger-woman relationships who were forced by circumstances to make hard choices. As you read of their struggles, remember the old axiom that says "we treat and judge others as we treat and judge ourselves." Don't be overly critical of them or yourself. The goal is to learn new things and try your best to work toward greater health and self-understanding.

Nick and Amy

Nick, a forty-six-year old engineer, and Amy, his thirty-one-year old girlfriend, had been together for over a year, and were planning on buying a house and moving in together. They were very much in love and Amy felt that, after a lot of searching, she had finally found a man she really connected with. Nick made her laugh, understood her viewpoints, and they enjoyed a mutual physical attraction that sustained their sex life. While Amy was a social drinker herself and had been with other men who behaved in the same way, she noticed early in their relationship that Nick was different. About every two months, Nick would go out with his friends and binge drink. After a while Amy could anticipate it. He would be vague about his plans and then, if she tried to contact him at all during the night, his cell phone was turned off and she could not reach him. Nick would come home early the next morning and spend the following day nursing a hangover. While this behavior pattern was not troublesome to Amy initially in the relationship ("It's a guy thing," or "There's no problem with a night out with your friends," Amy would rationalize), as they became more involved and began to live together, Amy became increasingly unhappy. There was one night when Nick did not come home and Amy was extremely worried about him. She told him the next day that if he did not at least contact her and let her know where he was when he had a night out with the guys, the relationship could not go on. She felt that if he was turning his phone off again and again, he may have something to hide and her trust in him began to erode.

It is important to state here that Amy was not a passive or shy woman. In fact, she was a corporate manager of a large distribution company and had numerous people reporting to her on a daily basis. She was confident and aggressive at work and in business in general. Nevertheless, the thought of losing Nick put her in the kind of emotional tailspin that left her feeling insecure, disoriented, and willing to live with the kind of behaviors she knew were not acceptable to her given her idea of a good relationship. Again and again, she had tried to explain to Nick that if he wanted to go out with his friends, she had no problem, but that when he became vague about who he was going with and where he was going, and then turned off his cell phone, she felt "ditched" at best and paranoid that he was trying to hide something at worst.

Nick made repeated promises that this would stop and acknowledged that Amy deserved better, but the behavior did not stop. It seemed to her that once he began to drink he lost perspective and accountability, and that if she were being honest with herself, she had to admit that this pattern would never really stop because she asked him to end it but only when he decided it should stop himself.

With her experiences dating and having relationships, Amy grew to understand that her idea of a good relationship, the kind she needed to be in to feel satisfied, required open communication and honesty. Most often this is what she had with Nick, except on those specific occasions. This is how she rationalized putting up with his behavior when thoughts of breaking up with Nick crossed her mind: She had what she wanted most of the time so she could live with his binges and all that came along with them.

This rationalization enabled Amy to continue on with Nick and avoid the pain she was so afraid of experiencing if their love were to end, yet it went against the grain of everything Amy knew to be true. In other words, she avoided acting on her own behalf, because it would hurt too much. Amy felt that to act on her instinct for self-protection would hurt too much, and she was stuck in a position of inaction. She began to feel a nagging sensation of the blues but couldn't really put her finger on it. As she went to the gym or the restaurants she and Nick frequented, as she listened to the country music she fell in love with when they first got together, Amy felt an empty sadness creep over her.

The final straw came one evening when Amy was out for a business dinner. She had driven to the restaurant alone and decided to pull out an old Squeeze CD that she never listened to anymore because Nick hated it. She blasted her favorite song over and over, as the music produced vivid visual memories of fun times in college. When at the table, the client called his wife to check in with her briefly. This crystallized for Amy the ideas that (A) she was not asking too much of Nick to let her know where he was; (B) that this was not a universal guy thing; and (C) that the overwhelming likelihood was that Nick would continue in this pattern and maybe even get worse. In one of the hardest moves she ever had to make, Amy broke up with Nick and endured the pain that followed. She was able to do so in large part because she felt good enough about herself as a person and a girlfriend, and was therefore hopeful that she would find another relationship. In the end, she felt strong enough to opt for the legitimate suffering required to move on, over the self-destructive suffering that would shelter her from leaving Nick.

Jamie and Sean

Jamie, a forty-year-old mortgage broker, grew up with an alcoholic father. Her parents were divorced and when her mother left her father and moved across the country, Jamie, then thirteen, felt as though she had inherited the role as his caretaker. Jamie did not want to leave the only home she knew and her lifelong friends behind to go to California with her mother, and so she lived with her dad while finishing school. In addition to pouring liquor out of bottles into the garbage behind his back, Jamie did their wash, kept the house clean, and often cooked meals for them. She felt as though if she could keep it all together, eventually her dad would realize that he needed to stop drinking. She managed to do pretty well in school, but felt a burning need to get out into the workplace instead of going to college. Jamie settled on getting an associate's degree from a local college while working in a real estate office. She quickly climbed the ladder at work, getting her real estate and then broker's license and then going back to school while learning the mortgage business.

Jamie was driven, independent, and often cynical about what she perceived to be men's unreliable, irresponsible, and immature behaviors. She silently vowed never to make the same mistake her mother did in marrying a man who used alcohol to avoid dealing with his pain and problems. It was at her fortieth birthday party that Jamie met Sean, a fifty-one-year-old divorced dentist with two teenaged daughters. They hit it off instantly. There was physical attraction and they had a love for active sports in common.

Initially, Jamie loved that Sean was dependable and responsible. It was a huge relief to finally feel attracted to a man she didn't have to rescue time and again.

Things began to deteriorate between Jamie and Sean. Jamie noticed that she frequently tried to provoke him into fights. She was unaccustomed to the lack of a cycle of angry or anxious feelings leading to the relief of reconciliation. This latter realization is one that Jamie made in therapy. When she and Sean came very close to breaking up, Jamie realized that her behavior was self-destructive and largely responsible for possibly ruining the best relationship she had ever experienced. She has since been in therapy working on discovering how her childhood shaped her choice in men and her familiarity with an unhealthy dynamic.

In this case, self-preservation required that Jamie tolerate the unfamiliar feeling of putting herself first and not totally sacrificing herself to a man. The experience of being cared for and being treated with equal importance was confusing and anticlimactic. She and Sean are still together.

Lisa and Eric

Lisa, a divorced thirty-two-year-old administrative assistant, met Eric, a forty-three-year-old producer, at the studio where they both worked. Eric had never been married, but Lisa was divorced and had custody of her five-year-old son. Neither wanted to quit their jobs, but neither was able to ignore the attraction they felt for the other. Lisa was impressed time and again by Eric's business savvy, his confidence with other top television executives, his success in the entertainment industry, and by his firsthand knowledge of culture from a lifetime of world travel.

After a year of dating while working hard to negotiate possible pitfalls during business hours, and getting used to being all together with her son, Lisa and Eric decided to take the next step in their relationship and move in together. Lisa was very happy, even as she found that her job as administrative assistant had evolved into that of personal assistant to Eric.

Once she had attained a good deal of knowledge, however, Lisa began to feel unsure that working in the television industry was what she really wanted. While she used to feel that she was living her own life as a working mother, Lisa began to feel like her life was only now an appendage to Eric's life. But her new life was chock full of new luxuries. There was extra time and much more money for clothes shopping, manicures, lunches with friends, and great vacations with Eric. Still, Lisa felt an increasingly strong need to reclaim her life and her identity as a separate person with a separate life and pursuits which defined her as an individual.

When she first met Eric, the tasks of keeping up at work and taking care of her young son pre-empted her chances at career advancement. Now she had a better life financially. Having been divorced once already, Lisa also had a strong desire to feel self-supporting and be able to give her son a good life, should things with her and Eric not work out. It became clear to Lisa that in order to reclaim her identity, she would have to give up the shopping, lunches, and vacations in order to get herself through culinary school, an old passion she had closeted after giving birth to her son. Because Eric was supportive, Lisa was able to help him find and train a new personal assistant and go through the necessary changes and effort to enroll in culinary school.

Losing Yourself in a Relationship with an Older Man

In Jamie's case, she was so used to forfeiting her own personal needs, that she was lost and even turned off at times by Sean's ability to love her without having to depend on her and impinge on her freedom to be an individual. Because she had good friends who provided a strong enough support network, she was exposed again and again to the idea that her father's demands were unfair and that he was suffering from an illness she would never be able to control. As a young woman this role made sense to her, but later on she could not break free of her father's dependence. When she almost lost Sean, however, she realized it was time to seek the help of a therapist.

For Lisa, self-preservation and expression of her identity came at the cost of relinquishing the kind of life and material benefits she had longed for but was unable to achieve given her status as a full-time working mother. Ironically, once she had them, she realized that these material things didn't make up for her feeling second-in-command to someone else, and losing the identity and sense of control she had had as a single woman struggling to make ends meet. Lisa realized she was lucky to find a man as generous as Eric but that she had to take the opportunity to work hard and go after her dream of being a chef.

Given the closeness of love and the high level of involvement in each other's lives, combined with the integrity of ones' own selfhoods when entering a relationship, people are at different degrees of risk for a romantic relationship to impinge seriously on their identities. In relation to others, there is a constant and ongoing shift between "them," "we," and "me" that requires good balance. Loss of identity can happen to anyone in the context of any relationship, but because of the caretaking nature of women's roles in relationships and in family life, women are especially vulnerable. After all, the very establishment of a "self" may be seen as "selfish" and is at odds with the constantly implicit and explicit messages received from significant others and society. It is said time and time again that to be a good girlfriend, wife, or mother, women must engage in self-sacrifice as they fulfill the wishes and needs of their loved ones, even at the expense of being themselves above everything else. The best-case scenario for any couple is one in which there is an allowance for the existence of two selves, two identities. Neither is forced, then, to betray himself or herself deeply and chronically to ensure the survival of the relationship.

For a woman, losing herself is quite feasible because of several factors in the older-man/younger-woman dynamic. You may even be at greater risk of loss-of-self if you are a "super caregiver" who is easily attracted to the older man who needs your energy and physical strength.

From the standpoint of age and life experience, there may be an exaggerated built-in position for each of them depending upon the age difference: he being dominant and she being subservient. While this idea may seem to run counter to current perceptions of the new younger woman who may be in her thirties or forties and is established in her career, old stereotypes die hard.

From a financial standpoint, there is the potential for grossly unequal distribution of wealth and power. From the perspective of a values system, and depending on his age and the era in which he grew up, he may have more traditional values, which are characterized by expectations that your first responsibility is to care for him, and your career is second to his. Because of his background, personality, and the qualities he desires in a mate, he may really just want a woman who "dabbles" in this and that during the day and is available for him in the evenings and on weekends. An established older man with a more traditional upbringing may not be used to a career woman who isn't readily available to fit into his schedule and life. The kind of partner he needs isn't to be found on a level playing field, ready to build the basic blocks of life anymore; and it's in building those (e.g., home, community social connections, joint wealth), where women have an opportunity to continue to establish their own identities as adults.

Don't Be Sidelined

If you are dating or in love with an older man who is already established, your agenda regarding your life path and your relationship may be different from his. It may, in fact, be difficult to clarify that while the two of you are still in that initial stage of "infatuation-love." Even if your agendas are not that different and you want to be the next Martha Stewart for a man who appreciates just that, you don't have to make a career out of satisfying his and only his need for comfort. To be sure, it is in the action of pursuing your own dreams and honing them that you grow, become whole, and feel the great pleasure of mastery—the great pleasure of true independence.

Be Suzy Homemaker because it fulfills your identity, because the activities and pursuits inherent in being Suzy Homemaker are consonant with all that makes up who you are, and because being Suzy Homemaker brings you joy. Pursue whatever your personal dream is, but don't get bulldozed into sidelining your goals, professional or otherwise. Whether you are twenty-, thirty-, or forty-something, you are at an important stage in your life. A stage in which you need to choose and perfect your craft, not meander around spending someone else's money in pursuit of immediate gratification. Women have critical stages in which they refashion their identities. It is precisely at this point of disarray and change that they are more vulnerable to losing what they've accrued to the temptation of a ready-made life.

The stability and success of your career are protective. The stability and development of your support networks and social circles are protective. They are protective of your identity. In your twenties and even thirties, you are still forming your identity, and a relationship with an older man, especially if he's in mentor or supervisory roles, can impinge on your identity. Beware the older man who feels threatened by your successes at work or by devotion to your career. Based on his statements and actions, you must ask yourself if he is being supportive or undermining. Some men are conflicted and can feel both proud of their girlfriend's accomplishments and threatened at the same time. Still others have the need for a younger woman to look up to and depend on him.

Sure, you'll not have to worry about having money to spend on a shopping spree when you sideline your career in exchange for his credit cards, but the immediate gratification of getting all the material things you want without having to make a meaningful contribution to the work force and society is short-lived and can become addictive. Feelings of emptiness and lack of control typically ensue when you are dependent on him to hand you money like a teenager asking for an extra twenty on the way out to the mall. Working toward your own goals (again the goals of housewife and mother are legitimate but take practice, hard work, and the development of real skill), makes the gift of a shopping spree that much sweeter.

The bottom line here is, stick with your pursuits. Don't lose patience and don't give up. If you're with a wealthy man, it's easy to get used to the valet and the gourmet take-out and the vacations. Even if you're not with a wealthy man, the life you build needs to be proportionately representative of who you are as an individual. Should it be over, you'll have to fall back on who you are and where you're going

The same is true with your social life. As in the case of your checking account, always have a separate one. Never lose sight of the importance of your friends and try to keep your finger on the pulse of their lives. True, you'll have one foot in each generation, but letting him become the focal point of your every move is an accident waiting to happen.

seven

Right Guy, Wrong Reason

A well-known psychologist in private practice once said, "When it comes to romantic relationships, we are either attracted to our mothers or our fathers." Obviously she meant that in the metaphoric sense; that is, that people are actually drawn to personality traits that are similar to those of their parents or childhood caretakers. To the extent that this is true, interacting with familiar personality traits in men recreates for some women some familiar interpersonal patterns and emotions from childhood in current relationships, and drives the way they experience and relate to each other.

Psychological Basis for Partner Selection: No, It's Not a Coincidence

There are several different principals from classical psychological theory that illustrate this very phenomenon.

Repetition Compulsion

Freud is the author of one such principal from classical psychological theory, which he labeled the "repetition compulsion." The repetition compulsion is a phenomenon from psychoanalytic theory in which people are driven to re-enact emotional experiences from early childhood without awareness or intent. Thus, women may find themselves inexplicably drawn to a man who has a constellation of personality traits similar to either their mother's or their father's. Over and over again they find themselves in emotional interactions with their boyfriends that mirror what they witnessed between their parents. How many times have you sat around and marveled at the eerie similarities between your significant other and a parent?

The Elektra Complex

Freud also described the "Elektra Complex," in which women experience a conflict similar to the Oedipus Conflict. In the Oedipus Conflict, boys have the unconscious desire to possess their mothers and do away with their fathers. Here, little girls struggle with the unconscious desires to possess their fathers and eliminate their mothers. In the traditional version of his theory, resolution of the complex happens when little girls make a solid identification with their mothers and rediscover their fathers—say in terms of their personality traits or style of relating—in a relationship with a mature man. Those eerie similarities to Daddy surface once again.

The Multigenerational Transmission Process

The "Multigenerational Transmission Process" is another phenomenon taken from family therapy. Murray Bowen, the author of *Systems Family Therapy*, describes it as the manner in which family members relate to each other emotionally—a manner that is transmitted within the family from generation to generation (say father to wife or father to daughter). As new spouses marry into the family and play their roles, they repeat and maintain these patterns of emotional relationships. Without elaborating any further on the technical part, let's just say it is quite likely that the men women choose as boyfriends/lovers/husbands will be predisposed to fitting into the emotional style of their families. In this way, they unwittingly maintain emotional issues or battles that were endured throughout their childhoods. Think back: How many times have you marveled at the eerie similarities between your relationship/marriage and your parent's relationship/marriage?

Object Relations

Numerous couples' therapists work on an "object relations" model, in which it is theorized that people unconsciously pick mates who remind them of those internal objects, or internalized versions of their parents, and relate to them with the same emotional patterns. Imago therapy is also a popular couples format, which postulates that the "imago" is a mental image of all the combined traits of the primary caretakers that reside deep within the subconscious. People then marry someone who has major similarities to their imago in an unconscious attempt to heal themselves by resolving the issues they had with their caretakers.

The OM as a Father Figure (Gasp!)

This section tackles the age-old daddy's-girl phenomenon as it applies to your relationship with an older man. In fact, research and theory support the idea that during early childhood, people start to observe how their parents interact and treat each other, examine each one's relationship with the other parent, and later use these observations in an evaluation process for picking future mates. Because children tend to identify with their same-sex parent, they then view the other parent as an example of what to seek out, or in some cases, what to go out of their way to avoid.

Research shows that attraction is wired into the brain early on. Apparently women become attracted to men with facial characteristics similar to those with whom they have had positive childhood relationships. In one such study, daughters who reported very positive relationships with their fathers tended to choose boyfriends or husbands with similar facial features. Pursuit of the similar facial characteristics may be designed to recreate aspects of the good relationship that was experienced in childhood. This same study showed that daughters who reported unhappy relationships with their dads tended to choose men who looked very different.

Another study in the area of father-spouse similarity has shown that women are actually attracted to men who smell like Dad! No, it's not Old Spice we're talking about here; more like pheromones, the chemicals that the body produces in order to communicate between the members of the same species. In the case of this study, scientists identified proteins on genetic markers and found that women preferred the smell of men who had certain genetic markers in common with their fathers and with themselves. In this case, the researchers say choosing men who smell similar to their fathers allows the women to pick men who share a selection of their own healthy genes, rather than risk mating with men whose fitness is uncertain.

Basic qualities such as feeling safe, loved, and cared for are sought-after qualities in a husband and father to your own children. And as the above research shows, Mother Nature has us using basic senses to gravitate toward those men.

> ♫ In everyday life, things aren't always simple. Practicality has to figure in to your choice also: Just think about that eleven-to-one woman-to-man ratio in New York City. One woman interviewed told us that her husband "is nothing like my father. . . . My dad was always easygoing and quiet, but my husband is intense and talkative. I would have loved someone like my dad but I never found one like him. We have a great relationship as far as I'm concerned, but we fight a lot about our son. I married the best choice I had. It's a practical choice."

There is also a lot of research that suggests that women who have bad relationships with their fathers don't avoid men who look or act like their dads. On the contrary, they actually seek them out. These women are actually more inclined to seek out men who are not good for them, and get into unhealthy relationships that mimic patterns from their childhoods. People tend to feel most comfortable with that which is familiar, even when the familiar is not necessarily healthy. This is especially critical for the girls who are making serious commitments when they are on the younger end of the spectrum. In their early to late twenties, women are probably less likely to be aware of the psychological factors that drive their attractions or the effect their relationships with their dads potentially play.

Maybe that explains why women with alcoholic fathers are attracted to alcoholic or addicted men, or why women with verbally abusive fathers end up in relationships in which their husbands harshly order them around or curse at them. Even women who are attracted to men who look like their fathers aren't necessarily aware of it until someone else points it out to them.

A patient of ours in therapy lost her father to a sudden and unexpected heart attack when she was fourteen. She explained that the man in her life, whom she loved dearly, was there one day and gone the next, and that she felt as though she had stopped trusting men, that is, stopped believing that they would stay with her. When she came to therapy, she had had relationship after relationship with men who were either unavailable because they were married, or unable and unwilling to commit to a relationship with her. These choices clearly mimicked a past, unresolved trauma and also served to reconfirm her suspicion that all men do eventually disappear.

According to Dr. Drew Pinsky, the well-known media psychologist, "If you have a horrible relationship with Dad, you are going to be powerfully attracted to horrible guys, and there's not a lot you can do about that by yourself. . . . If you tend to go for bad guys, and you're attracted to the same type over and over again, it's okay to think, 'If I'm really attracted to him, he's probably a bad idea.'"

While it's obviously not logical, neither is love. Often women feel drawn to a man by a combination of emotion and sexual attraction. That emotion may actually be a combination of the familiar feelings experienced in childhood toward fathers, mixed in with the sense and hope of a real resolution to the conflict she had with him, or Mom had with him, this time around. This cocktail of hope and sex seems powerful enough to make women think they are truly in love and literally compels them to be with this man. While a healthy love relationship has the ability of partners to understand and heal each other as one of its main components, this is different. When the initial sexual chemistry mellows, one can be left with a connection that is fraught with many of the same problems experienced firsthand in childhood. With enough awareness and a willingness to work in therapy, it's possible to break the cycle. We have had numerous patients come to therapy and cite as one of their main motivators the fact that they don't want their daughters watching and emulating an unhealthy marriage. It's possible to overcome an unwitting compulsion, but it takes recognition of unhealthy patterns in your choices of men and relationships and a real commitment to change, usually with the guidance of a trained therapist.

Recreating Dad or Running Away?

While women will often seek out a man who treats them as their father did, or who even shares similar physical characteristics, sometimes women will do exactly the opposite in an effort to avoid past pain. Does that strategy work? Without an understanding of past family dynamics and without real self-awareness, probably not. Running away from the problem with a lack of consciousness, perspective on childhood pain, and coping skills is no more effective than running headlong into the problem and recreating it.

The following sections, while oversimplified, are meant to be guides for you. What can you recognize from your past? What can you learn about yourself that you might apply to your current situation or patterns of choice in men?

These are examples of styles that create dynamics that can set a young woman up to be attracted to an older man with similar characteristics. She then loses herself in the battle of resolving old issues by taking on the archaic role of the daughter she once was.

FATHERING STYLES

Overprotective: He monitored everything you ate, wore, and watched, and everyone you socialized with, like a hawk. Nothing and nobody was good enough for you. This is a style that can instill fear and anxiety about taking reasonable and necessary risks in life. This is also a style that can breed the culture of victimhood. No matter who wronged you or why, they are the ones who are at fault; you are the innocent bystander in a world full of thugs.

Overbearing: He was overinvolved in your everyday life and an intruder in your emotional life. Maybe he projected his feelings onto you, insisted that he knew how you felt better than you knew, and went as far as making decisions for you that you were capable of making yourself. This is a style that can lead to a shut-down, withdrawal, or disconnection from your own feelings and desires to the point where you don't even know who you are, how you feel, or what you want. Doesn't everyone know a "selfless" woman who forfeits all of her desires and needs to satisfy us—the martyr? It's one thing to take pleasure in altruism and another altogether to do for others because you never found out who you are or you feel too guilty to do for yourself.

Absent: With or without the promise of being there, he was not. Feeling ignored, unloved, or not good enough to capture Dad's attention, a little girl is on a seesaw, bouncing between mistrust or hatred of men and an intense quest to capture their love and affection. If you find yourself with a man who is emotionally distant or just plain full of reasons to be unavailable, and you feel driven to get him to connect, to stay in one place, to accept you, and to love you, beware. Not many goals have the same kind of urgency. But wait a second, sit down, and have a real conversation with yourself about the pain you felt when your dad was not around or let you down over and over. Little girls typically think it is their fault that he hasn't come around, but thinking and feeling this way as an adult is relying on an outdated belief system. Adult women have the power to reframe their memories and get the fresh perspective that it wasn't ever really personal. It very likely wasn't your fault at all or your flaws; it was the result of his unresolved issues. Take a rest and give an available guy a chance. His very availability may seem foreign or even unattractive, but that may come from the old Groucho Marx feeling that you'd never want to belong to a club that would actually have you as a member.

Supercritical: Nothing you've ever done was good enough. This style can lead to chronic self-criticism, low self-esteem, perfectionism, and a battle of striving for unrealistic self-expectations versus low frustration tolerance and a tendency to give up altogether. If you've internalized this critical voice, it's likely haunting you in many of your pursuits or even daily activities. One woman we interviewed described her dad as a detail-oriented, obsessive-compulsive who was fanatically clean. Only now, in her forties, did she begin to realize that Sundays spent cleaning and re-cleaning the inside of the kitchen cabinets and refrigerator drawers have always been accompanied by a voice that described the food storage areas as "disgusting" and "a filthy mess." These were her father's words, not hers. She found that part of her internal voice was repeating the harsh critique over and over, which was spurring her on to clean in repetitive patterns. Here was an opportunity to start to combat that voice with a more reasonable description, one that is an actual estimate in the present day instead of an old obsession that wasn't even hers.

Angry: Whatever his other personality traits, his temper raged from zero to ninety in sixty seconds and you either walked on eggshells in an attempt to be invisible or rose up like a phoenix from the ashes to battle him back. Maybe you grew into a little hothead yourself, became adept at avoiding any kind of confrontation, or still have both tendencies living side by side within your psyche. While this dynamic can be recreated in any age scenario, it can be the younger woman literally taking on a guy close to Daddy's age in order to prove to herself that she can overcome him.

The "Yes" Man: He gave you everything you wanted. Maybe you had to whine, beg, flirt, and wheedle, but you got the toys, the clothes, the car, the college, the credit card, and so on. When you got into a mess with your high school teacher or the parking cop, he got you out of it. When you wanted a job with a certain agency or company, he had connections and, well, you got that, too. Here is the dad who, while having the noble impulse to give his daughter what she wanted, stunted her ability to endure pain, become comfortable with delayed gratification, or take pleasure in the rewards of her own hard work. That is an easy dynamic to recreate with a financially established older man, especially one who tends to be controlling.

Beware though, the tradeoff for his "allowance" can be a big one. You may forfeit many freedoms such as hanging out with your own friends, taking classes that you want, choosing where you live, eating out where you want, and so on. After all, you may be in a relationship with a guy who feels that it's his money, so you should do what he wants and be grateful for the nice lifestyle he's given you. It's one thing to evaluate your mate as a good provider for yourself and your children, but make sure it's about your love for him and not a tradeoff for your own adulthood. You will pay a steep price in a situation like this.

The Alcoholic: Regardless of other personality characteristics, he was a mess by many standards. Coming home late, coming home drunk or high, getting drunk or high around the house, losing jobs or relationships with friends and family, and having violent or loud arguments with Mom; in sum, doing a host of irresponsible and even dangerous things at a time in your life when you are being told by teachers and ministers not to cheat or lie, to be responsible, honest, and "just say no." While some women wondered what all the fun was about and began to partake in alcohol or drugs, or even just learned how to be really good sneaks or liars, others became the little parent: skipping the carefree part of childhood and moving prematurely into the state of lecturing him on his health, writing up contracts with him, or begging him to stay sober. You poured alcohol down the drain when he wasn't around, cleaned up after him, bailed him out of jail.

It's one thing to be a loving caretaker and another altogether to rescue someone over and over from the big messes they've created. It has been said that people acquire the jobs they take on, so be careful. If, at the outset of the relationship, you find yourself solving every problem and cleaning up every mess, watch out. While intuitively it might seem that this would not be the typical older-man/younger-woman dynamic, think again. Part of his attraction to a younger woman may indeed be connected to the feeling of safety and security that comes with knowing a younger, healthier, and energetic woman will be there to lean on for the long haul. Again, it's okay to give help and support, but when it's a 24/7 sort of job, it is not healthy.

The Stepfather: In our society, the word "divorce" is still a dirty one fraught with all the sadness and trauma that may accompany the breakup of a marriage and family. Research shows, however, that it is the ability to co-parent and low levels of parental conflict that are associated with children's mental health. To the extent that Mom's next marriage is a happy one, there is certainly the possibility that a stepfather may have provided Mom with a good partner and you with a role model for a healthy relationship, not to mention a loving father-figure. Obviously not all stepfathers ride in on a white horse and save the day, but they can offer peace where there was conflict.

The Loving Heart: He was not perfect, but you always have known that this man loved you unconditionally. This is the father who was really able to make his daughter feel loved and cared for. This is the kind of love that cultivates self-love. Becoming accustomed to feeling important and deeply cared for can create in you the ability to stand up for yourself in relationships.

The Martyr: He was always there for you and, boy, did he let you know it. Everything came with strings attached, of course. Ah, the heaviness of guilt and the lightness of running away. In this scenario, the daughter is made to feel heavy amounts of guilt for the slightest wrongdoing in any interpersonal situation. There are two possible roads to take here: the earnest attempt to live up to the impossible goal of being perfect in every social interaction, or the "duck and hide" persona who is always as superficial and as far removed as possible for fear of drowning in the guilt she perceives to be constantly coming her way. For her, the older man is quite possibly the man to be taken care of, and alternately to be left behind as she runs off with her peers as an escape.

This is too simplistic. This takes learning to listen in the moment and being able to bear the reasonable criticism or hurt feelings that come in every relationship without beating yourself up to the point that you want to run away and have no intimacy at all.

These are examples of styles that create the dynamics to set a young woman up to be attracted to an older man with similar characteristics. She then loses herself in the battle of resolving old issues by taking on the archaic role of the daughter she once was.

> ✿ What are the memorable characteristics of your dad? We interviewed a number of women in relationships with older men and got the full gamut of answers:
>
> *He made me feel safe.*
>
> *He made me feel important.*
>
> *He was tolerant, physical, supportive, funny.*
>
> *He was intimidating, hotheaded, condescending, patronizing, absent, supercritical, undependable, a workaholic.*

Case Studies

Is it chemistry or familiarity that draws us to each other? The following case studies have been adapted from clients in our private practices.

Danielle

Danielle described her father as "obsessed with manners and ashamed of my body." Danielle, who already felt self-conscious because her body had developed much earlier than her twelve-year-old peers, was criticized frequently for wearing clothing that was too revealing, yet she felt she was in fact dressing like a typical teenager. There were many battles waged over what she wore and deeply hurt feelings when her father made negative comments about her outfits. She reported feeling angry and a still harbors a sense of shame she has not been able to shake. She is married to a man whom she describes as also "conscious of my appearance and insists that I do not go out of the house without makeup."

Margaret

Margaret's parents were divorced when she was only four, and her father was awarded custody. He thought that his second wife had been too harsh and demanding on Margaret and felt a tremendous amount of guilt for that and the divorce as well. He compensated for her sadness with material gifts, and by the age of six he described Margaret as an unhappy, unruly, demanding little girl whose tantrums were only temporarily quelled by giving her the gifts and toys she wanted. Margaret came for therapy feeling empty and unhappy in a marriage where she got all the material goods she wanted, yet somehow felt lonely and unfulfilled. She derived a sense of herself as being worthy or loveable from getting material gifts and from showing them off to others. Her husband fed into this dynamic and complained about being the caretaker while Margaret underfunctioned and then felt she was being treated like a child. Now, as an adult, the loneliness she felt had begun to outweigh the satisfaction she once got from acquiring material things.

Lori

Lori's father passed away from a sudden heart attack when she was thirteen in the 1970s. Her mother was left with a family business to run and she was "baptized by fire" as Lori described. Her mother was also a beautiful woman who was pursued on a regular basis by numerous men. Lori recalled her mother loving the attention yet feeling overwhelmed with grief and feelings of abandonment at her husband's death. Her mother soothed herself by reveling in the attention of men and dating a lot. This left Lori to "keep it together emotionally for (her) mother" and herself. She described feeling like the mother as she frequently reminded her mother to be home by midnight and worried about her on her various dates.

In essence, Lori had assumed a parental role on an emotional level and never got the opportunity to grieve the loss of her father with the love and support a child her age needed. By the time Lori reached her fifteenth birthday, she became sexually active and then began to take tremendous pride in the attention from boys her age and older. As she sought out their attention, she became an increasingly effective seductress, although she never felt emotionally satisfied. For years she pursued an emotional connection on the basis of sex. After her second divorce, in therapy she realized that she had spent a long time unwittingly trying to heal her own feelings of abandonment and grief by modeling an unhealthy strategy on that of her mother's.

The Power Play

Be on your guard if you begin to hear the following statements come out of your OM's mouth:

- "One day, you'll understand."
- "When you get a little older you'll know what I'm talking about."

- "Oh, never mind, it's something that happened in the 1980s; you wouldn't remember."
- "I know better."

Sound familiar? It should, because these are statements a father says to his daughter, not those a boyfriend says to his girlfriend. Depending on your age difference, it's very possible that your older man occasionally fights the urge to condescend to you. If he has fought the urge, maybe it's because he cares about you and your happiness, and wants to crush every single stereotype surrounding men who date younger women. If he fails to repress this urge and points out your shortcomings frequently or in public, he is trying to control you by fashioning himself as a father-type figure. While people do tend to "mother" or "parent" each other in relationships, it's a matter of degree. Remember he is not there to be an authority figure; he is there to be your equal partner.

Men can have power trips at any age, but it's easier to play the daddy role when he's, well, your daddy's age. While the manipulation may not be physically threatening or emotionally abusive, it's much harder to find happiness and prosperity in a relationship where the scales are tipped in his favor. If he is always right, and always in the know, then where do you stand? What could you possibly have to say that he hasn't already studied and commented upon? A few more months of "Honey, let me explain it to you so you understand," and you'll either wind up a scared mute, walking on eggshells, or you may just blow your stack at him with an intensity he never imagined. While it's not a reason to ban all older men, it's a great reason to get rid of this one.

Some men thrive on manipulating their significant other, and it's difficult to draw the line when your man's weapon of choice is maturity, experience, and worldliness. Some indicators that this relationship is headed into father/daughter territory are:

- You would rather keep your mouth shut during a discussion because he'll argue over whatever you say and win. After all, he'll insist, he's usually right.
- He proofreads your master's thesis (or presentation for work, or newsletter for the PTA) without your even asking.
- He corrects your grammar way too often.
- He turns every discussion into a debate and never backs down, even if it's about something trivial.
- You are having gut reactions to him that are eerily similar to those you experienced when you were with your father in those same situations.

I Love You, You Love Me. Let's Change Each Other!

The battle from childhoods past rages on between partners who subconsciously use the relationship to wrestle down and conquer old demons. With a genuine attraction for each other, commitment to change, and the guidance of a trained couples' therapist, it can be accomplished when difficult issues are coming up and not just "going away" on their own.

Does all of this necessarily mean that your older man is some phantom re-creation of daddy? Not at all. In fact, self-awareness and perspective on our childhoods help build a good relationship no matter what your ages, and if your man happens to be a good decade older but you feel genuinely happy, loved, and cared for, go for it!

eight

His Medicine Cabinet

If you open his medicine cabinet in search of an innocent Q-tip, don't be shocked at the number of products and medications crammed in there, many of which you, as a younger woman, don't recognize. Depending on how much older he is, and his luck of the draw with genetics, you may hear about medical problems, physical concerns, and plain old vanity issues you never did with your peer boyfriends. It's not only that with age come wear and tear, but also that men these days are fighting tooth and nail to feel as virile as their twenty-something competitors. "Aging well," "defensive aging," or not aging at all is the goal. We are now living in a culture that does not see growing old as a natural process, as part of the human condition, but as a "problem" to overcome. Hence the bottles, tinctures, pills, and gel caps—many of which are related to his sexual health or other health-related issues that directly tie into his feelings of masculinity.

Sexual Performance

Your fella probably falls into one of two categories when it comes to sex: (1) He's realistic about his stamina, but consoles himself knowing quality is better than quantity; or (2) he longs for his twenty-five-year-old erection, despite the rest of his body being forty-, fifty-, or sixty-plus.

℞ People age sixty-five and older consume more prescription and over-the-counter (OTC) medicines than any other age group, according to the National Institute on Aging.

Sexual performance is the number one concern of men who start dating again after a long-term relationship. The advent of Viagra in 1998 has helped many men gain the sexual confidence it takes to pursue younger women. The irony is that most women (as you know) say that the ability to listen, take cues, engage in foreplay, and give clitoral stimulation is much more important to their sexual satisfaction than penis size or hardness. Nevertheless, somehow at Viagra-inspired hour four, you start getting sore and worried about lack of sleep and the workday ahead, and you start wondering how much of the evening's sports have to do with his wanting to relive his twenties and how much has to do with the intimacy that builds a relationship.

Sexual Dysfunction

In the short time since its approval, Viagra (or the newer Cialis or Levitra) has become a household word, so the probability of finding an erection enhancer in his medicine cabinet is as high as there being aspirin or Band-Aids—whether for diagnosed impotence, erectile dysfunction, or "recreational" purposes (when he has a long special evening in store).

So what you can expect from your OM when it comes to sex? Research shows that as men age it takes longer for them to both produce a full erection and to ejaculate. They have a decrease in the force of ejaculation, and an increase in the duration of the refractory (recovery time) phase. Testosterone patches may offer a solution, and in some cases, his doctor might suggest other ways, such as penile vacuum pumps.

> 🐾 If your man hasn't tried Viagra, chances are he's curious about its effects. In one focus group we performed for girlfriends of older, erectile-enhancement drug-free men, respondents voiced the wish that their partners would try an enhancement medication—sometimes for the physical "benefits," but more often in the hope that it would lessen his sexual anxiety. Go figure.

A study on sex and older adults published in the *New England Journal of Medicine* found that despite these changes, the pattern of sexual activity doesn't seem to change dramatically compared with previous studies of younger adults. In other words, among those who were sexually active, the frequency of sexual activity was two to three times a month or more. So what that suggests is that if one has a partner, the frequency of sexual activity doesn't change a whole lot across age groups. Both men and women were more than twice as likely to have engaged in sexual activity in the past year if they considered themselves in excellent or very good health, compared with those who described their health as fair or poor.

So, while the incidence of sexual dysfunction increases with age, sexual dysfunction is primarily related to an increased rate of overall health problems, rather than merely getting older. Factors that affect sexual function include: cardiovascular disease, diabetes mellitus, dementia, arthritis, and surgery. Medications that affect the autonomic nervous system, such as antihypertensives (for high blood pressure), tranquilizers, and antidepressants, may also adversely affect erectile function and libido or sex drive.

> ✍ If you find herbs such as ginko biloba and ginseng behind his bathroom mirror, he's probably taking them in an effort to enhance sexual function. Those creams? Vasodilators: They increase the blood flow to the penis; however, watch out—many need to be washed off before penetration. If he does try them, make sure you read the small print carefully.

Changes that occur in the sexual physiology of an aging male can affect both erectile function and ejaculation, but this doesn't have to have a functional impact on the subjective enjoyment of the sexual encounter. Knowing that these changes aren't catastrophic may be crucial in preventing dysfunction due to performance anxiety.

Regardless, despite anxiety centered around sexual and medical problems, most older men said their decline in sexual activity year after year was due to the lack of a partner. Enter you.

Sexual Health

A recent study from the University of Chicago published in the *New England Journal of Medicine* presents an image that researchers say runs counter to the stereotypes of older guys as either asexual or "dirty old men." Based on data collected from 3,005 adults ages fifty-seven to eighty-five during two-hour, face-to-face interviews from July 2005 to March 2006, the findings show many are sexually active as long as they're healthy.

🕊 Approximately 250 million people in the world have diabetes, a disease that in men can cause erectile dysfunction or impotence ten to fifteen years earlier than men without diabetes. The statistics are alarming: 35 to 75 percent of men under fifty; 50 to 60 percent of men over fifty; and 95 percent of men seventy and older with the disease have difficulty achieving an erection.

In the preceding twelve months, 73 percent of those fifty-seven to sixty-four; 53 percent of those sixty-five to seventy-four; and 26 percent of those seventy-five to eighty-five said they were sexually active. Among those who reported good or excellent health, 81 percent of men and 51 percent of women said they had been sexually active in the past year. Of the oldest sexually active respondents, 54 percent reported having sex at least twice a month; 23 percent reported once a week or more. According to one study 59 percent of married men in their seventies still have sexual intercourse with their spouses. The most common reason for sexual inactivity among both men and women was a male partner who had a physical health problem, the study found.

It's All in His Head

Problems with your OM's sexual performance aren't necessarily related to erectile dysfunction. Changes in his appearance might affect your guy's emotional ability to connect. As he notices more wrinkles and gray hairs, he might feel less attractive. A poor body image reduces his sex drive because he doesn't feel worthy of sexual attention. The stress of worrying too much about how he'll perform can trigger impotence. Men who have experienced erection problems may become so anxious about inadequacy that they start to avoid sexual situations altogether. Other psychological factors, including depression, lowered self-esteem associated with the onset of physical signs of aging, and substance abuse, can all contribute to the problem. In addition, chronic pain or surgery (such as prostate surgery) and illness that may cause fatigue can make sexual activities more challenging or even painful.

The Good News and the Bad News

First, the good news: Older men, even if they aren't retired, are likely to have more time for romance and intimacy, and are usually more relaxed than the younger men you've dated. Older men are also less likely to have premature ejaculation. That *is* good news.

The bad news? Older men are more likely than you might think to have a sexually transmitted disease, including HIV/AIDS. In fact, recent media has reported higher-than-expected STD rates in both older men and women. This statistic may be due to the influx of older adults returning to the dating pool with outdated knowledge on how to protect themselves from disease and limited experience with putting on a condom.

> 🦅 Ask him to get screened as soon as possible. No matter how many times you've broached the topic with a partner, it's hard. Be simple, clear, and matter-of-fact. Reassure him that urine tests have replaced the dreaded swab and just saying "full STD screening" encompasses everything from HPV (genital warts) to HIV.

About 10 percent of all people diagnosed with AIDS in the United States—some 75,000 Americans—are age fifty and older. Moreover, because older people generally don't get tested for HIV/AIDS on a regular basis, it is likely that there are more cases out there than documented. Older

Americans know less about HIV/AIDS than younger age groups for a variety of reasons, including:

- Health care workers and educators have neglected educating the middle-aged and older population on HIV/AIDS prevention.
- Older people are less likely than younger people to talk about their sex lives or drug use with their doctors (and doctors tend not to ask their older patients about sex or drug use).
- People age fifty and older may mistake HIV symptoms for normal aging. It can take as little as a few weeks for minor flu-like symptoms to arise or ten years or more for more serious symptoms to occur. Symptoms may include headache, chronic cough, diarrhea, swollen glands, lack of energy, loss of appetite and weight loss, frequent fevers and sweats, frequent yeast infections, skin rashes, pelvic and abdominal cramps, body sores, and short-term memory loss.

He may have seen more of the world than you have, and have a better financial portfolio, but when it comes to sexual health, STD screening, and protection, you are the pro. Don't forget that.

Father's Little Helper

When taking Viagra, men must have realistic expectations. The drug is not an aphrodisiac; it does not change libido or desire. The message of Viagra (or Cialis or Levitra) in many TV ads is that it can give older men back the lost manhood of their youth. But your guy should also know that there are possible side-effects: headache, flushing, indigestion, nasal congestion, mild and temporary visual changes (blue/green color perception changes, light perception changes, and blurred vision), diarrhea, and dizziness. Also, that Viagra must be taken one hour before anticipated sexual activity and on an empty stomach.

> ✍ A sixty-three-year-old Long Island woman sued her seventy-year-old common law husband for $2 million, "claiming that, upon obtaining a Viagra prescription, the man had promptly started running around with another woman."

The most important contraindication (and really the only major one) for Viagra is when a patient is also taking nitroglycerin. Just as the seventy-year-old penis isn't what it used to be, neither is the seventy-year-old heart.

How Does It Work?

The smooth muscle in the human penis (the cylinder called the corpus cavernosum) contains compounds called PDE receptors, and specifically, the type-5 receptor, which is responsible for creating an erection. In brief, when nitric oxide is released from nerves within the corpus cavernosum during sexual stimulation, it activates an enzyme called guanylate cyclasa. This enzyme helps elevate the level of cyclic guanosine monophosphate (cGMP), which, in turn, relaxes the cavernosum tissue, allowing an erection to occur. Viagra, then, prevents the breakdown of (cGMP), which produces an erection, thereby prolonging the erection and even inducing its occurrence in men who would otherwise be impotent. Even simpler? Viagra causes blood vessels to relax so that more blood can flow through them (this causes the erection).

Born-Again Dad?

If you'd like to be a mom, or be a mom again, you may wonder about the quality and quantity of your older man's sperm.
Research finds that men who delay fatherhood too long put
their children at higher risk of inheriting genetic diseases. A
study published in the *Archives of General Psychiatry* in Sep-
tember 2006 found that mutations in the sperm of men over
forty could be a contributory factor to a significantly higher
risk of having children with autism. Concurrently, researchers from Mount Sinai School of Medicine, New York, found
that men over forty have a much higher chance of fathering
children with autism, compared to men under thirty.

In another study, researchers analyzed gene mutations
and other types of DNA damage in sperm samples collected
from ninety-seven healthy California men between the ages
of twenty-two and eighty. They found that the likelihood of
acquiring a genetic mutation that causes a type of dwarfism
increases by about 2 percent per year, beginning in a male's
mid-twenties.

Sperm Production in Older Men

A gradual decline in fertility is common in men older
than thirty-five, in part because of a decrease in testicular
size and sperm (or testosterone) production, and decreased
force of the ejaculatory squirt. In young men it is often powerful and can eject the sperm some distance, but it is much
less in older men, which means an increased distance that
the sperm must travel upon ejaculation.

Regardless, many couples are finding success in fertility treatments and alternative plans like adoption. More on
babies and new family dynamics in the next chapter!

Hair Matters

Baldness is a touchy, if not life-altering, subject. In our experience, next to diminishing sexual performance, balding (or thinning hair) is the second most traumatic experience for aging men. Psychosocial effects have been studied both in the United States and abroad.

Your man may play it cool by saying, "Hair? Whatever," with a roll of his eyes. But when you're not looking, he's probably craning his neck over the sink behind a locked bathroom door in order to monitor his increasingly enlarging bald spot. He might even take daily stock of the grays now sprouting in double digits, and verbally threaten his diminishing hairline, as if instilling fear in those front men will keep them from running away. Wearing a scarf or a skullcap like an aging rock star would never go over in the office and he has too much pride to one day go to work wearing a toupee.

The University of Iowa Health Care reports that one man in four begins to go bald by age thirty, and two out of three men are completely bald by age sixty. Most experts agree that 85 percent of men have significantly thinning hair by age fifty. Male baldness can vary, depending on heredity, hormones, and illness; nevertheless, though myths abound, hair loss is 95 percent genetic, and can start as early as sixteen, or never at all.

𝔰𝔟 Many men lament that as they lose the hair on their heads, other parts of their body get hairier, and excess or coarser hairs grow in the ears and nose.

Common baldness is often called "male-pattern baldness," but the medical term is "androgenetic alopecia." The earliest stage of real male hair loss is characterized by a recession around the temples. During the next stage a continuing thinning may be accompanied by hair loss on the crown. At this point, there's still a solid band of hair across the top separating the front of the head and the bald crown on the top of the head.

Most guys hope it will stop there, but unfortunately, once it's started, it rarely slows down. The band or bridge of hair eventually disappears, leaving a dramatic single large bald area on the front and top of the scalp, while the hair on the sides remains relatively high. This is when men resort to comb-overs and baseball hats, depending on job dress codes. Perhaps the most dreaded stage is the George Costanza look—when a horseshoe-shaped fringe of hair is all that remains on the back and sides of the head.

> ♬ Straight from the man's mouth: "Everything else I've been able to either fix or cover up. I broke a tooth and had a veneer put on, I lost my gut by working out . . . it seemed like it was from one day to another that my hair started looking thin. I couldn't stop thinking about it. It dampened my morale from one week to the next. I'm constantly being tempted by those hair ads. Part of me tries to console myself and say that it's about what is inside, but I know women like a full head of hair if they have a choice."

We don't need studies or polls to tell us that receding hairlines are one of the most traumatic situations a man can face—it ranks up there with diminishing sexual function and job loss. With baldness comes psychological stress, loss of self-esteem due to change in appearance, and being perceived as older than they really are. The billion-dollar hair loss industry proves that men not only care about hair loss, but are also willing to spend whatever it takes to prevent it. The amount of money spent on male hair-replacement pills, capsules, gels, camouflage sprays, mousses, massage therapy, and hair transplants leaves little doubt.

Despite the fact that there is not one FDA-approved product that promises to regenerate hair to its original natural state, you may still spy at least one of these products in your guy's cabinet:

- Rogaine (and other brands using a solution of minoxidil, such as Avacor)
- Proscar (and brands using finasteride, such as Propecia)
- Procerin
- Advecia
- Hair Genesis

Avacor, the most popular hair-restoration product on TV, claims a 90 percent success rate. It uses minoxidil and a hodgepodge of other ingredients, including ginkgo, horsetail, bilberry, and saw palmetto. It is fairly expensive, too ($500 to $1,000 a year), and needs to be used daily. Other less popular solutions require massaging into the scalp, and stress the importance of good circulation.

ƒ❧ Bald Guyz products are very successfully sold to the unhirsute (or follicularly challenged). They specialize in things like "headwipes" and sunscreen. The company was born in 2005 in response to their findings that 35 million U.S. men are in some stage of male pattern baldness, ranging from about 20 percent in their twenties to about 65 percent in their sixties. Hair restoration is a $1.7 billion-a-year business.

The men's hair grooming market gets bigger every year. Hair color for men seems to be only whispered about, but the industry is sizzling: sales reached over $100 million last year. In these modern times, though, hair color for men is marketed for maintenance—that is, to cover middle-aged gray in an effort to look younger. The image of a youngish-looking man gradually regaining his dark locks by simply combing Grecian Formula through his hair and building up to the desired color is a familiar commercial. Few men actually change the color of their hair to take on a totally different look the way women often do; however, if a man wanted too, he'd most likely simply use women's hair color. George Clooney and Anderson Cooper are leading the pack of powerful men who are embracing their gray-toned hair and proving how attractive and distinguished the look can be.

So much ridicule has been heaped on hairpieces and comb-overs that many men have chosen to go *au naturel* by shaving their heads and growing facial hair. If your man is sporting this take-control style that mimics Bruce Willis, Moby, or Michael Jordan, you may find quite a stash of electric buzzers like Norelco or German Dovo straight-razors under the sink.

If your guy takes the "distinguished gray" route, call his hair "gun-metal gray" or compliment him on his perfectly shaped buzzed head to give him an ego boost. Make sure to mock Fabio, Trump, and any other hair-obsessed man.

The Male Menopause

Between the ages of forty and fifty-five men may experience a phenomenon known as andropause, which is characterized by a drop in testosterone. (During menopause, women experience a drop in estrogen.) The bodily changes occur very gradually in men and may be accompanied by changes in attitudes and moods, fatigue, a loss of energy, sex drive, and physical agility.

Testosterone Replacement Therapy (TRT)

While the media's coverage of steroid use may make it seem like everyone's doing it, chances are you won't find any anabolic steroids or syringes in your older man's medicine cabinet.

As a man ages, the amount of testosterone in his body gradually declines. This natural decline starts after age thirty and continues throughout life. Adequate testosterone levels are important for maintaining muscle bulk, adequate levels of red blood cells, bone growth, sense of well-being, and sexual function. If you run across testosterone patches or gel in his cabinet, it may have been prescribed to him for erectile dysfunction. There have also been studies that show there was significant improvement in cognition seen for spatial memory, spatial ability, and verbal memory in older men.

Other causes of lowered testosterone levels include:

- Injury, infection, or loss of the testicles
- Hemochromatosis (too much iron in the body)
- Dysfunction of the pituitary gland (a gland in the brain that produces many important hormones)
- Medications, especially hormones used to treat prostate cancer and corticosteroid drugs
- Chronic illness
- Chronic kidney failure
- Liver cirrhosis and alcoholism
- Stress

Growth Hormone

Your body naturally makes growth hormone to help fuel growth during childhood and to help maintain tissues and organs throughout life. However, beginning around age forty, the pituitary gland—the pea-sized structure at the base of your brain where growth hormone is made—slowly reduces the amount of the hormone it produces. Reduced growth hormone results in loss of strength and energy, increased body fat (especially around the abdomen), and psychological changes.

The dwindling level of growth hormone may be responsible for the frailty that is typically associated with getting older, which has prompted some to turn to injections (by prescription only) of synthetic human growth hormone (HGH) to stave off the realities of old age. There's little evidence, however, to suggest that the human growth hormone is, in fact, the silver bullet for staying young. The only clearly positive effect found from taking the hormones was a slight improvement in lean body mass. On the negative side, participants who took human growth hormones were significantly more likely to develop joint swelling and pain and carpal tunnel syndrome.

Nonetheless, through studies of adults with growth hormone deficiencies we do know that injections of human growth hormone can increase bone density and muscle mass, decrease body fat, bolster the heart's ability to contract, improve mood and motivation, and increase exercise capacity. Stimulating the production of growth hormone in healthy older men and women may, consequently, return hormone levels to those found in younger adults and reduce body fat, according to research conducted at the University of Washington and the Veterans Affairs Puget Sound Health Care System in Seattle. These results provide more fodder for those who believe that synthetic human growth hormone can help healthy older adults who have naturally low levels of growth hormone regain their youth and vitality.

Mental Health

Researchers estimate that each year depressive illnesses affect one in eight U.S. men (more than 6 million in total). Often men and the family around them don't recognize clinical depression because they expect to see sadness rather than the anger that is more common. Compound this with the myth that older adults are naturally "grumpy," and it's understandable how depression in older men is often overlooked.

Common antidepressants are:

• Selective serotonin reuptake inhibitors (SSRIs) such as Celexa, Prozac, Paxil, and Zoloft
• Tricyclic antidepressants such as Elavil, Norpramin Sinequan, Tofranil, and Pamelor
• Selective serotonin and norepinephrine reuptake inhibitors (SSNRIs) such as Effexor and Cymbalta
• Your man may also be trying to help alleviate his depression with herbs and supplements such as St. Johns Wort

The most common mental health problems are classified in a group called "Anxiety Disorders," which include panic disorders, phobias, generalized anxiety disorder, obsessive-compulsive disorder (OCD), or post-traumatic stress disorder (PTSD). If your OM has suffered from any of these, you might be looking at a bottle of Klonopin or Ativan. These could be for anything from occasional panic attacks to fear of public speaking.

🐾 Although older adults comprise only 13 percent of the population, they account for 20 percent of the suicide deaths in our country. Depression is the foremost risk factor.

Sleep Problems

Sleep patterns change with age: Older adults spend more time in the lighter stages of sleep and less time in the deep, restorative stages. For many years, benzodiazepines—so-called tranquilizers such as Valium (diazepam), Halcion (triazolam), Xanax (alprazolam), Restoril (temazepam), and others—were prescribed for insomnia. The "new" sleeping pills are Ambien (zolpidem), Sonata (zaleplon), Lunesta (eszopiclone), or Rozerem (ramelteon). If he is going the non-medication route, you might find some melatonin or valerian in his cabinet instead.

Digestive System

If your man has a digestive disorder, he's certainly not alone. Nearly 40 percent of all older adults experience one or more symptoms each year, largely due to the changes that occur in the digestive tract with age. A 2005 study found, however, that a gastrointestinal problem is also the number one side effect (number two was fatigue/dizziness) of heart disease medications, pain relievers, cholesterol-lowering drugs, antidepressants, blood thinners, sedatives, antibiotics, water pills, narcotic pain relievers, and drugs used for stomach or intestinal problems.

Seven basic symptoms can alert you to your guy's gastrointestinal tract upset: nausea, heartburn, vomiting, bloating, pain, constipation, and diarrhea. Sometimes these symptoms will be diagnosed with a well-defined disease or condition (Crohn's, Celiac disease, Ulcerative Coliti, gas, acid reflux, peptic ulcers) or a food allergy.

More than 16 million prescriptions for digestive problems were dispensed in 2005. Antacids, or acid blockers, sold under brand names such as Axid, Pepcid, Tagamet, and Zantac, are among the most popular medications prescribed in the United States to treat ulcers, acid reflux, and other gastrointestinal disorders.

🐾 Herbs and supplements that can help with digestive problems are: Aloe vera gel, vitamin C, quercitin, glutamine, bicarbonate, hydrochloric acid, charcoal capsules, and aloe vera juice (with lemon).

Prostate Health

The prostate, that walnut-sized gland that makes and stores semen, is located just below the bottom of the bladder and in front of the rectum. Because of its location, and because it becomes enlarged as a man ages, the prostate creates some very incommodious urinary problems. More than half of sixty-year-old men and as many as 90 percent in their seventies and eighties have some symptoms of benign prostatic hyperplasia (BPH), so depending on the age of your man, it's likely he'll have some medication for this condition in his medical cabinet.

Some common OTC formulas include Super Prostate Formula, Prosvent, Beta Prostate, and Prostate Miracle. Most contain combinations and varying amounts of saw palmetto, lycopene, pygeum, zinc, stinging nettles, alanine, blycine, and clutamic acid. If you see drugs with these ingredients, your fellow has probably had a PSA (a test that measures prostate specific antigen, a protein produced by the prostate) and has a PSA level of 1.5 or higher.

Only if the situation becomes dire with symptoms such as a hesitant, interrupted, or weak stream of urine, urgency, and leaking or dribbling, and more frequent urination (especially at night), will a visit to the doctor be necessary. At this point, one of two types of prescription drugs will be prescribed: 5-alpha-reductase inhibitors (5ARIs), which improve long-term symptoms and may reduce the need for surgery, or alpha-adrenergic antagonists (alpha blockers), which relax smooth muscle cells, help improve urine flow, and reduce uncomfortable symptoms.

TMI, right? We know.

nine

Is He Ready for Marriage?
Don't Count on It

A re you just assuming that an older guy is looking to settle down because, well, that's what all people are all supposed to do eventually? Are you frightened to broach the topic? Are you anxious he'll say no or maybe even yes? Even with all the advances women have made, it still seems like this dance transcends time and feminism—and it's usually a Sadie Hawkins dance.

> 🐾 "73 percent of the women coming out of marriage license bureaus with their future husbands told us that they put pressure on their man to get a proposal. In most cases, this pressure didn't involve an attempt to manipulate their man into marrying them but was simply a result of telling their man what they were feeling." John T. Molloy, *Why Men Marry Some Women and Not Others: The Fascinating Research that Can Land You the Husband of Your Dreams*

As current literature tells us, and as we've already pointed out, from birth girls are wired to process and use heaps and heaps of language on a daily basis without feeling taxed.

165

Women are also wired to anticipate and attend to the needs of those who pull at their heartstrings. If you're a mommy, it's your brood (and hopefully your husband); if you're a not a mom, it's your man. If you have no man it can become the cats (well, they need love, too).

Regardless of who or what kind of pet is the lucky beneficiary of your love and care, you tend to want to invest your time and energy into something long term. You've put a lot of time, effort, planning, and thought into creating and maintaining a good life with him. And despite the divorce statistics and the frightening stories on daytime TV about infidelity, marriage is still a goal for many. Maybe it's about the ring, maybe it's about the formality of the document, maybe it's about the ceremony, maybe it's about the vows. We won't judge.

Newsflash: Just because he's older and has been through more, don't assume he'll automatically share your marriage aspirations. For various reasons we'll discuss, he may not.

> ♫ His brain does not comfortably process the reams of language that a woman's brain so effortlessly does when "relating" in the intimate sense, whether to a friend, sibling, lover, or spouse. He tends to get satisfaction from side-by-side relating versus our face-to-face analysis. The sexes bond differently; in fact, attempts at "bonding" with them in the classic female style of intense, face-to-face interaction can lead to a cataclysmic shut down. Ever watch their eyes glaze over as you try to explain how the relationship can work better?

Now on the flipside, when you go into this relationship, you may even find yourself surprised or confused by your own reaction to the prospect of getting hitched. In this day and age, it's more acceptable to openly express your real desires. When talking to women about their desires for the future, we're finding that lots of childbearing-age women are very satisfied with a life without a formalized "husband" and children.

So whether you feel mother-nature spurring you on toward the marriage-with-kids finish line, you know you want a committed relationship but want to take one day at a time, or you just feel plain confused, here are some guidelines for action and self examination that will hopefully light the way.

Jaded by Divorce? Still Fearful of Commitment?

In keeping with this biologically driven relationship model which preserves the species through genetic variability, a man is looking to spread his DNA by having multiple relationships/liaisons/babymamas or whatever you want to call them. In short, from a biological perspective, we are apparently at odds when it comes to marriage. His taking a "spread the love" approach, if you will, versus our full and ongoing investment in one man, one family, one life.

In going into this relationship you might have assumed he wanted to get married. He either never has (and what is he waiting for?) or his been separated or divorced for a while, and you think, well here you are: the chance to do it right.

Lend an Ear

Has he been well-trained or traumatized by his former relationship(s)? If you've found an older man with the ability to articulate his feelings and to actively listen to you, then perhaps his ex-wife, his girlfriends, or even his mother did a good job priming him for relationships in general, and you may have a guy who also takes pleasure in being in a long-term, stable, committed relationship. If he has learned female social protocol (e.g., how to just listen sometimes and give empathy instead of solving your problem, or remembering to tell you he loves you or that you look pretty, or taking the time to also listen to how your day was) this is a great beginning. If he was traumatized by repeated rejection stemming from some already deficient relationship skills he brought to the table, he may have gotten more and more gun shy, less and less able to communicate with a woman, and more and more confused about, or avoidant of, long-term commitment.

Rule number one is to listen. When you're sharing about your lives and experiences with each other, really listen to his words. Did he love his ex? Is he bitter about the split and can't shake his feelings of anger? Does he acknowledge his part in the split? Has he been able to forgive her for her mistakes or hurtful actions? What does his attitude about risks seem to be? What are his ideas or values when it comes to marriage? Are his parents still together? What is his perception of their happiness with respect to the marriage? What did either or both of them gain, endure, or forfeit in the name of staying together; and, in his opinion, was it worth it?

Here's an important thing to remember, though: Flaws do not make him a bad guy or not worth staying with. The real question is, is the mix of your personalities such that you bring the best out in each other and are you both getting enough of what you need to feel genuinely happy? Husbands and wives can spend lifetimes working on flaws or even learning to live with and accept them if they feel happy and satisfied enough in the marriage.

If your goal is marriage and a family, don't hesitate to talk about exactly that. (Hint: Use those exact words, not euphemisms or metaphors.) You don't have to bring it up over appetizers on your first date, but definitely do so early on. Older men or men who have already been married are typically ready to have this kind of discussion and factor it into whom they date. And even though there are a lot of older men who are just not ready to get back into marriage so soon because they've been through a terrible divorce or only recently become divorced, they will hopefully 'fess up and want to make that clear. Some, on the other hand, have spent the last years of the marriage feeling so lonely they might yearn to be coupled again soon. At the very least, if they don't articulate it, their actions will speak for them soon enough.

Regardless, the name of the dating game at this point has a lot to do with efficiency. Neither men nor women typically want to go on a treasure hunt for those open to marriage and kids, or worse, be strung along. Life is short. Most are willing to be up-front instead of coy about marriage and family. The question is, how has his past affected him? Is he taking advantage of lessons learned and gaining new understanding of himself and relationships, or is he getting too stuck in the pain he felt and walking around in a defensive or confused state?

You Do and He Doesn't

He was married once (or twice) and he ain't going to do it again. He's one of those guys who firmly believes that marriage ruins a relationship. Maybe he's looking at the relationships around him and marriage doesn't seem to work. He says he'll commit, but he just won't do it like everyone else. Or maybe he's licking his wounds from his past relationship and it is going to take a long while. Whatever the situation, make sure he is clear with you, and more important, that you are clear with yourself.

> 🐾 "Going through my first divorce was hell. I will never put myself or anyone else through that. I will make vows, even financial agreements, throw a party to celebrate our love, whatever . . . but go through that again? No way. I learned."—John, 49

He Does and You Aren't Sure

Despite the fact that he's ready to buy the ring, you're not so sure. Here are just some of the reasons that may be causing your hesitation.

Career Concerns

"I feel like if I get married, it will make me lose focus on my work, and right now is a critical time in getting where I want to be professionally," says Melanie, thirty-four. Sure enough, vocational experts warn that taking "time off" and going back to work may not be as feasible as once thought. The worry about "falling out of the loop" is valid and depends on how fast technology changes within your field or the average age of someone in your position.

> 🐾 A recent news report illustrated that corporations are wooing women back to the workplace with flex time and the ability to work from home. This is an attractive option for lots of women who want to "have it all" and be with their kids as well as keep their jobs.

Since the age and experience range of the modern version of the "younger woman" has broadened in recent years, it really is a very heterogeneous group. While some "younger" women are divorced and already have children, others are frightened of giving up a chapter in their lives, and want to put marriage off.

Widow-Phobia

What if he dies way before me? I don't want to have to deal with that! Not marrying him doesn't mean you won't miss him if you break up. Besides, forty-year-olds have died of sudden heart attacks and anyone, at any age, can get hit by a bus. There are no guarantees in life but feeling happy in a loving relationship in the present moment is worth a lot. Same goes with concerns about nursing him in his old age. The point is that there are too many unknown variables, so have that conversation with him to make a plan, weigh your options with a clear head, and move on to enjoy your life today.

Baby Issues

He wants to get married and wants kids. Or, he wants to get married and doesn't want kids. He's definite about his feelings on the topic, the problem is you aren't (or you don't agree).

In Her Words

"We are talking about marriage. Most things we agree on, it's so nice. When it comes to kids he is very frank, he doesn't want any more. I'm not sure about it. I feel like if I marry him I will cut myself off from something I may want later on. . . . "

Marianne, 28

Have this conversation up front really soon. Make sure you consider all the alternatives. Whatever you do, don't give up your dream unless you feel strongly about it, and don't think you will change his mind eventually.

Either he's been there done that, or wants to be together as a couple and has no interest in adding to his partnership with you. This is one of the most difficult relationship decisions our patients have experienced. You love the man but being with him means the future the way you envisioned it won't include children. Is he worth giving that dream up for? Can you weigh the good, the bad, and all the uncertainties and come up with a response you can live with?

The question here is, can you grow together in places where you're on the level with each other, and can you feel okay to go out and finish the business of your youth without feeling like you're betraying, or being looked down upon, by your man?

Signs He Is Interested in Marriage

While there can be similarities here between younger men and older, more experienced men, there seem to be indicators that transcend age. Generally speaking though, if an older man is ready for marriage (whether he's divorced or not), moving toward that goal often happens more quickly and directly. Here are some indicators to be aware of.

1. **There is a high degree of trust and familiarity between you.** You've met his family and closest friends. His "private" life has become decreasingly private and he shares a lot with you (fears, embarrassing moments, dreams of the future). He is open about things such as

friends, family, and finances. If he's an intensely private person, opening up and sharing information may come very slowly but you will see a continuous trend in that direction if you are getting closer.

2. **He's proud of you and you know it.** He's proud to be seen with you and proud to introduce you to his family and friends. Granted, he may not be running around screaming this in the town square, but still, you sense that he is happy to have you meet and be around his close friends and family members.

3. **His biological clock is ticking and he makes it known.** Lots of men, too, get antsy about the prospect of being an eternal bachelor. At some point in their lives (no particular age cut-off here), they start to think the party's over and focus on finding the right woman to settle down with.

4. **As a couple, you have the financial resources to make it work.** Whether he makes more money or you do is irrelevant; it's that (whether you are putting your resources together or keeping them separate) there is no huge financial problem that will put stress on the relationship.

Signs that You Need to Move On

For starters, if you've been together for at least six months and you're not seeing any of the indicators from above, it may be time to think about ending the relationship. Or, if the opposite of any of the above is true and he's often secretive about important things having to do with his friends or family, or if instead of showing his pride in you he's busy trying to make you over, then it's time to move on.

If you've attempted to discuss marriage with him and it hasn't gone well, there are two likely scenarios you must face: either you've attempted to discuss marriage and/or future plans and he's been continuously avoidant, or you've discussed it and he's openly stated that marriage is not for him.

🐾 Researchers at the University of London found serial relationships are good for men's mental health. Break-ups are painful for both sexes, but more so for women, who generally take longer to recover. Women's mental health becomes progressively worse the more break-ups they have, and the more new relationships they start. The study, published in the *Journal of Epidemiology and Community Health,* also suggests that men who stay single are most likely to suffer depression.

In the first-case scenario, you may have a man who needs more than six months in a relationship to really talk about your future together in terms of marriage, and that's fair. It's difficult to speak in terms of hard-and-fast time deadlines, but when you've been together for about a year and he's still avoidant of this conversation, it's fair for us to advise you to move on. In the second scenario, you need to be accepting of his statement, period. If you are ignoring his lack of desire, or trying your hardest to change it during the course of your relationship, you need to do some serious soul searching and ask yourself why. Are you avoiding breaking up because you're scared you won't find a "better" guy? Are you caught up in using this relationship to "fix" an old unresolved issue you had with your dad—or with your mom, for that matter?

Last, but certainly not least, is your evaluation of the relationship. Even if he is ready, do you really want to marry this guy? Remember, a marriage is a partnership and, as such, you need to be able to work well together as a team. You don't necessarily have to be similar in nature or personality, but you do have to be able to communicate well with each other, and you do have to treat each other with the basics. "Basics" means you do your best to treat each other with kindness, respect, and empathy. If this means that you need to go to couple's counseling before the wedding, don't assume that you're doomed. Learning how to communicate effectively is invaluable and many couples need to learn and have refresher courses throughout their marriages. Finally, don't operate under the false assumption that getting married will make other problems vanish. Getting married will probably make them worse!

For Love or for Money?

Based on our interviews, there are pretty much three camps when it comes to feelings regarding love and money. The practical (i.e., the gold digger), the romantic ("I'll take love and poverty over money, any day"), and the realist ("I want love *and* money"). The majority of women, however, seems to fall into the latter two camps, with love being a core reason for them to follow through and marry their boyfriends. In the first case, the temptation is very real for women who have always had to struggle to make ends meet and pay the bills on their own, or for women who grew up around wealth and have expensive tastes for things they can't always afford.

Some women are quite blunt about their fantasy of wanting a really older man with a lot of money and a boyfriend on the side. Sounds pretty mercenary, huh? You might not like this woman but if one of her core issues revolves around feelings of inferiority and a compulsive need to keep up with the Jones's in order to preserve a shred of self-worth, at least you can feel sorry for her. Put in a softer light, though, how often have you or friends daydreamed about the freedom to go shopping on his credit card, not have to work if you don't want to, and never worry again about money? In the end, this is often no more than a daydream and a blunted impulse, and the idea of a marriage built on money alone is unappealing to many women who are already well developed enough to want a partner they can actually relate to. The purist describes this situation in all-or-nothing terms and will say something like "I'd choose love and poverty over emptiness and wealth," but the two things are not mutually exclusive and it is possible to make an effort to date men who are better providers.

If you happen to fall head over heels in love with a man who isn't currently financially stable and doesn't really have a lot of prospects, that's okay—just as long as it's genuine love and not a re-enactment of the caretaker coming to the rescue of the wounded. By the same token, two people can be drawn together by what initially seem like shallow factors such as looks or money, but who says that can't develop into genuine love? After some experience with dating and relationships, it may become clear that features such as kindness, generosity, sense of humor, and financial security are just as legitimate to pursue as sexual chemistry. Eventually the chemistry changes; it doesn't necessarily go away altogether and there are plenty of ways to reignite it, but it never stays exactly as it was in the beginning. Truly, you are left as two human beings living together and problem solving as a team. Who do you want on your team? Again, it's experience with relationships that can provide these lessons in a concrete way.

New Roles?

In spite of Mother Nature's powerful forces, modern society and technology have made it easy for a reversal of the traditional picture. These days we have more independence, more money, and more childbearing years. This seems to have spawned a breed of urban woman who now, in her late twenties and throughout her thirties, is experiencing the same protracted adolescence that was once typically enjoyed by men. Even if you don't feel this way all the time, admit it: There are some good long moments when you are happy to know the top is always down, you can sleep in as late as you want, pick up and go as long as your job allows, and don't identify with Bridget Jones at all. Enter the older man.

With your orientation centered around career, freedom, travel, and the powerful feeling brought on by good business savvy, you guys are probably like a couple of peas in a pod when it comes to daily living. Maybe more like best friends with sexual attraction than the classical Ozzie and Harriet duo, your relationship is getting a boost from the mutual understanding of what it is to have a hard day at work and a concrete understanding of the value of a dollar. This new arrangement has you both working and both dealing with household chores, even if you are a big consumer of laundry service and take-out.

While this lifestyle may be all you've ever known (and although you want to get married one day, it's not today) a woman with this lifestyle could really throw an older man for a loop, especially one who has been married since the 1960s or 1970s. Roles have clearly been redefined here. His comfort zone is more about being in a marriage and maybe this time around it's he who wants to tie the knot and you who is avoiding the tradeoff of a career for marriage and babies. If all you've known is peer relationships and the guys around your age were evasive, avoidant, and panicked about "getting serious," the experience of a boyfriend actually feeling more comfortable about marriage can feel really strange to you. Maybe you can take the opportunity here to reframe what felt like rejection in past relationships with younger guys and now walk a mile in their shoes.

ten

Troubleshooting

Everyone knows that the best way to deal with a problem is to nip it in the bud right at the beginning. The second best way is to avoid it all together. To help you along when the going gets rough, we've put together our top troubleshooting recommendations based on the multitude of older-man/ younger-woman couples we've seen. This chapter covers all the major problems a couple can face, from the complexities of infidelity to simple arguments about daily life.

Taking It Slow: Get to Know the Man Before You Jump into Bed

This suggestion truly involves a tug-of-war of epic proportions in the human brain between the ventral tegmental area and the caudate nucleus (the parts of the brain that get stimulated and charged up by the release of "lust/love" hormones and neurotransmitters) versus the frontal lobes (the uniquely human part of the brain that helps people evaluate what they're doing and make rational choices). When in the throes of lust, waiting-to-be-physical may be the last thing you want to do, but surely it is the best way to know what you're getting into and with whom. After all, chemistry is not synonymous with compatibility. Remember that once you have sex, you start to have expectations about certain behaviors; for example, how often you'll communicate; who will pay for what; where the relationship is heading; which plans with whom take priority; and so on. In essence, premature sexual intimacy is sort of like buying a car over the phone. You haven't really seen it, driven it, or had the chance to customize your options. So there's a good chance that before long you'll want to trade this one in for a better ride.

Think older men are wiser about it? Perhaps they are more experienced, but they still fall prey to the same deeply rooted neural circuitry that drives women into sex with the objects of their affection. This is clearly illustrated by the fact that HIV is on the fastest rise among the sixty-plus set. The seniors may not be wise regarding safe sex, but apparently they're busy. Not that that's a bad thing; it's known that sex is actually good for one's health. Studies also show that older men (fifty plus) enjoy sex as much as when they were in their twenties, flagging erections and all! So don't leave the big decision up to your older man; he may be just as impulsive and irrational about the whole thing as your twenty-something variety of boyfriend.

Remember, Mother Nature has put together some great "feel good" lures to encourage procreation—namely the biological drive toward love and the orgasm. According to biochemists, love is comprised of three distinct states: lust, attraction, and attachment, with the latter, attachment, predominating in more enduring, committed relationships. Lust is governed by a potent cocktail of hormones, including estrogen or testosterone. Attraction is driven by neurotransmitters called monoamines, which are structurally similar to the amphetamines that stimulate the production of adrenaline in the body. (Adrenaline is responsible for that heart-racing good feeling that comes over a person when attracted to another.) The attachment phase is characterized by more mellow feelings and the drive to "nest." Oxytocin and vasopressin are hormones that are an integral part of breastfeeding. So find out who this man is before you jump the orgasm gun. Be aware that, with an orgasm, you get a spike in dopamine, and the feelings created by excess dopamine are those that are associated with falling in love romantically with a man. That dopamine rush can even trick you into believing that you're falling for a guy you had casual sex with. With orgasm, you also get spikes of oxytocin and vasopressin, both of which are associated with feelings of deep attachment, so you can feel an intense union with a man after sex. This intense union, in reality, has not yet been established via more everyday routes or experiences. Hence the whole "love is blind" phenomenon—it's likely that you are not going to really see this guy clearly until the neurochemical effects have worn off and, by that time, you may already be walking down the aisle (yikes!).

Signs You're Ready to Do the Deed

While there is no ideal timeframe for waiting to have sex, here are ways to measure how well you know this guy and how comfortable you are in terms of pursing a more serious relationship:

1. You consider yourself comfortable enough to have candid conversations about issues pertaining to sex such as: which form of birth control and protection against STDs you prefer; what has or has not worked in past

relationships with respect to sex; and what you would do in the event of an unplanned pregnancy.

2. You have become familiar with the typical way in which he handles responsibilities: from big ones (such as work commitments) to smaller ones (such as making sure to call you about plans—in advance). Ask yourself: Does he shy away from or seem to resent responsibilities and obligations or does he handle them without being evasive or giving others a guilt trip?

3. You've had ample opportunity to see how he treats others: both intimate (e.g., friends and family) and casual (e.g., waiters and coworkers). Is he a tease? Does he give compliments? Does he give put-downs? Does he seem to recognize the way in which another person might feel about or see a situation?

4. You have become familiar with the way in which he handles commitment in general and the fulfillment of promises. Does he tell a lot of white lies to get out of obligations that are not fun or does he rigidly stick to prior commitments, even when the current situation calls for change?

5. You have observed and possibly even been on the receiving end of tactics he uses during conflict. Is he a fair negotiator? Does he become controlling and demanding? Is he able to recognize his contributions to a misunderstanding that ballooned into a fight? In your estimation, is he very defensive and unwilling or unable to hear and see the others' points of view?

6. You have seen how quickly he loses his temper and what behavior ensues. Does he get frustrated quickly and easily? When he does, does he yell, take the floor, and not let you (or anyone) get a word in edgewise? Does he storm off in a cloud of anger?

7. You have a sense of what it's like to share things about yourself and your life with this man. Does he listen? Sounds like a tall order, but with time and varied experiences—such as more than going out to dinner and having sex; seeing a movie and having sex; or just plain having sex—you can learn a lot about a man.

Oops! I Did It Again . . .

What's a sexually active girl to do when in the middle of a battle between her head and her, um, less logical side? The overwhelming rush of lust can turn even the most rational, objective, and unflappable of women into idiotic daredevils. One study, called "Sex on the Brain," asked men in love whether they'd take an immediate $15 or wait for a guaranteed $75. The men said they'd take the $15 *now*! You do the math, girls. Their impulsivity made them more apt to settle for 80 percent less dough. According to anthropologist and love expert Helen Fisher, when in love, people become less inhibited, more daring, and high on adrenaline. When she interviewed men and women in the throes of romantic love and asked what percentage of the day and night do they think about their beloved, the answer was "all day and all night." When she asked if they would die for them, the answer was, "yes, easily, yes."

> ♪ Only abstinence and condoms will provide you with effective protection against STDs such as gonorrhea, syphilis, genital herpes, human papiloma virus or genital warts, and HIV/AIDS. Moreover, spermicides with nonoxynol-9 have been shown to decrease the incidence of HIV spread. And don't assume that just because you didn't have sexual intercourse you're protected. Oral sex can also lead to the spread of STDs.

Not to squash romance, but this all sounds like the perfect formula for impulsive, imprudent decision making to those of us living in our heads. In spite of all the advances made by women in western society, they're still living with that whore/Madonna dichotomy. Hence they still deal with the old "I slept with him . . . I'm so bad" guilt trip women lay on themselves (no pun intended). In this scenario, an older, more experienced man can be a breath of fresh air, and actually be a part of the process of slowing the pace—if he's open minded and wise enough to understand that he needs to get to know you as well. In fact, this guy may be the one fending you off! Either way, while some guilt may be productive enough to help you control yourself, too much guilt is never a good thing. So in the end, while it is better to hold off if you can, there's no sense in beating yourself up if you don't. But do, *absolutely do*, use protection!

So if you have "gone for it" on the early side, you must realize that you are now driving through a rainstorm—complete with heavy fog and bad wiper blades. In short, it is that much harder to see what you're up against, and whether the destination (i.e., the relationship) really looks habitable. That's not to say that you won't get through this period in one piece or that things won't work out. We're just talking about increasing the odds of establishing a relationship with a man you actually like and decreasing the odds of catching a nasty bug down there.

In sum, if you have jumped the gun, don't beat yourself up but do *learn* from your mistake. Become aware of what drew you to him and what you didn't see clearly about him (see Chapters 6 and 7). You *will* see the situation that much more clearly on the next go-round if you make a conscious effort to focus on errors. If you just sit around, kick yourself, avoid looking at your behaviors, and try to go 180 degrees in the opposite direction with the next guy, you'll be riding the mistake merry-go-round for a while.

When He's Dragging His Feet on that Divorce

This is a tricky one, and the reasons for the "dragging" are the ultimate factor here. Possibilities include:

- He's gotten cold feet about leaving his wife and the security of his old familiar life.
- He's overwhelmed by the prospect of a contentious divorce and the impending financial losses and/or obligations, including alimony and child support payments.
- He's feeling uncertain about how you and he will work out as an enduring couple, and is having a recurrent fantasy (make that nightmare) that he may go through the same divorce with you down the road.

Getting involved with a "soon-to-be-divorced" man can be much like having an affair with a married one. It can be an emotional rollercoaster when he's pulled in two different directions and feeling confused and guilty. One minute you may be the center of attention while at other times you take a clear backseat to his former life. To an extent, this is the case with any older man who has been married to and/or has a child with another woman. The difference, though, is that an already-divorced man has waded through and negotiated the treacherous territory of alimony, child support, bitter custody battles, and so on, and you have (fortunately) entered the scene after some ground rules have been established. Moreover, he has hopefully come to terms and achieved resolution before meeting you, and there is a carved-out space in his life in which you are more readily able to fit.

Best advice: Don't drag your feet with him for too long. We don't want to give hard and fast rules here: You'll know when you've had enough. Even if you have strong feelings for him, you may need to step away from the relationship and invite him to contact you when he feels ready to get involved and build a new life with you in the picture.

The Accommodation Syndrome

Remember all that adrenalin, vasopressin, and oxytocin pouring into your system with the advent of attraction and attachment? This potent combination can turn the most ordinary career-oriented modern girl into Martha Stewart on steroids. When you first fall in love with him, washing his underwear can be "cute"! All of a sudden you have the intense craving to be with him, to cook for him, to clean for him, to type up his invoices, to make the bed, to fluff the pillows, to buy that special kind of peanut butter, to get him water in the middle of the night, to pick up his dry cleaning. In short, to take care of him as if he were both a lover and a child. And because women are hardwired to be caretakers, they become super-caretakers when their brains are marinating in all these neurotransmitters and hormones. What we're calling the Accommodation Syndrome is what occurs when he becomes accustomed to your abundance of care and you get stuck in the supercharged version of yourself that happens at the outset of love.

What happens after a year or so of this when the neurotransmitters and hormones begin to die down and the demands of every day life set in? A disappointed boyfriend is left wondering what happened to the mint on the pillow, the extra-fresh laundry, and his favorite recipe for dinner every Tuesday night. Of course they're not all the same and they, too, realize what's happening. Nonetheless, watch out if your man expresses entitlement, dishes out too much guilt, or you yourself are prey to guilt about this change.

Best advice: Don't go overboard on the loving care, and by all means, do *not* forfeit your desires or let your endeavors take a backseat, assuming that things will work themselves out. They don't. Set his expectations at a realistic level from the get-go. Sure, it's nice to go out of your way for him and to be flexible, but don't forget yourself in the process.

How does your older man fit into this schema? If he's been in a long marriage, he may be used to having his wife take care of all the aforementioned things, whereas a younger guy today may be used to having his mother do it. For the older man, your efforts and care may mean a tremendous amount to him, especially if he's balancing his life with you with an ex-wife and children.

What Are Our Expectations for Fulfillment?

Never lose sight of this: "A man is *not* a woman with XY chromosomes." They don't think like women, walk like women, talk like women, or *love* like women! They're different creatures altogether. Remember that the love of your life will never be the same kind of friend or companion as a female friend or sister. It just doesn't work that way, and the sooner you accept this fact, the greater chance there is for harmony. To help you along, here are some of the most common expectations that set women up for heartache:

He will be your "best friend" and satisfy all your social/emotional needs. No, he really won't and that doesn't make him bad. While women actually get a rush of dopamine and oxytocin from just talking and connecting (yeah, remember that's what happens with orgasm, too), men don't crave long talks, to say the least in some cases! You need a varied support system complete with girlfriends and family members (provided that you have one or two you really connect with). Men and women are different "animals." To be sure, research has shown that as testosterone peaks during a man's adolescence, there is a decrease in talking and interest in socializing—with the exceptions of sports and the pursuit of sex! The nice thing with the older man is that testosterone levels decrease with age, which in combination with more relationship experience can lead to a more expressive guy. Of course it will also help greatly if you are generally happy with yourself and your life (see Chapter 6).

He'll change if I'm really persistent and even drag him to therapy. Well, perhaps he'll grow and become a better version of himself, but you must remember one thing: It will happen only if he wants to change himself! We cannot emphasize this enough! Good news though: With the same drive and persistence you use on him, you can change yourself and your own ideas, assumptions, feelings, and behavior.

"Love will keep us together." Again, no, it won't. If you're a romantic and believe that love will automatically rule over differences in values, personalities, and even age, it likely will *not*, which brings us to the next myth . . .

Once you fall in love, that's it, it's always there. This is *not* true! Love is work. When you love deeply, you invest your time, energy, and thoughts. Keeping the love alive involves real effort at times: doing things you don't want to do, giving energy that you don't feel like giving, and so on. And a lot of the work involves self-evaluation and renovation. An older man can be practiced at exactly this kind of work and be a great partner in these efforts.

How to Fight Fair

The top issues couples fight about are money (what to spend it on, how to save it, how much is enough, what "thrifty" means, and what "generous" means), sex (how, when, where), chores (from your own messiness to food shopping), children (yours, his, whether you'll have some together, how to raise them if you do), and time (what should be done with free time, how much is too much work time, and what you should do with your downtime).

Being with an older man may change what you argue about, as compared to disagreements with your past peer-aged boyfriends. Maybe you've struck gold, and your older man has more time and money, doesn't mind doing chores, likes sex as often as you do, and, if he has children, you have a nice relationship with them. Maybe, more realistically, one or two of these topics is exponentially worse because he is older. Which ones ring a bell for your relationship?

When listening to our patients describe the topics they'd fight about, we heard things like, "Jonathan had never done chores for himself, ever. When it came to dividing up who did what, he just assumed I would do it all like his ex-wife did, but I sure as hell wasn't taking up that role. I work, too!" and, "While Jason initially had time to see me, it seemed time got tighter and tighter. He had to spend time with his kids and he had a demanding work schedule. It seemed like we only saw each other to eat and sleep. I felt like I had to fight to just be with him!" And as we've already mentioned, the older man who lavishes time and money on the younger woman is not so pervasive in real life.

A majority of men who have divorced over the age of fifty were left by their wives, so chances are you are dealing with someone who is not new to anger or arguments. Though he probably has more experience arguing, this sure doesn't mean he can do it more effectively. While some men will argue at age forty or fifty the same way they did at age twenty, there may well be some differences. Lori (thirty-six) told us that, "My last boyfriend, who was a year younger, would argue for hours but Stan (fifty) just shrugs, says okay, and then does what he wants to anyway, it's infuriating."

Another patient reported, "His ex-wife would get really mad and stay mad, so John is not scared of my temper. If I raise my voice or get emotional, he understands that I need to vent in order to move on and he lets me go longer than my younger boyfriend ever would."

So, depending on the fighting repertoire created by his past experiences, if they were good or even varied enough, it is very possible that he has more skill in this department than your younger guy.

How Do You Fight?

- We try to listen to each other, but it usually deteriorates because our views are so different.
- It escalates quickly to really loud talk and from there turns into full-on yelling! We both feel attacked.
- We both bring up old stuff that is not related and it gets totally exasperating.
- I usually end up crying—more out of frustration than sadness. He either shuts down or gets even madder.

- It starts in different ways, but always ends up with, "If you don't _____, then it's over."
- We go back and forth and I end up with my feelings hurt and feeling isolated.
- As soon as there is discord, one of us walks out of the room.
- We argue about one thing, when it's really about built-up tension from something totally different.

Get out of the Ring

Men are wired to compete and to dominate. They love competition, be it the intellectual competition of debates or the head-on collision of UFC ultimate fighting. We've told countless patients, "Don't get in the ring with him. Help him get out of the ring to talk to you." How do you do that?

The first thing to do is remember that women and men process anger differently. Feelings of anger are generated in a very specific part of a man's brain, which may be why they can turn it on and off so easily. Conversely, since women are "wired" to keep the peace and avoid conflict, his transgressions build up over time before you finally lose it. And when you do, it involves your whole brain: memory, verbal, emotional. Consequently, simmering down can take exponentially longer and involve a lot more analysis and debriefing.

We find that when couples come for counseling, many of the women spend a large percentage of the "fight" trying to make their significant other understand how they feel. For men, it's more often about being right or wrong; there is less premium placed on "that Oprah stuff" (quoting one of our more obstinate patients). Remember, men have less experience articulating their emotions and less ability to hear feedback. Another critical point is that, for some men, compromise may be akin to accepting defeat; just listening to your point of view is akin to giving up his own. Do your best to acknowledge his points while calmly standing your ground. At the end of the day, a good session involves really hearing each other's feelings and points of view, and then problem solving. It can be difficult, but once you get into the pattern of doing this, you'll find heated arguments that go around in circles happening less.

Take these tips:

- Don't threaten each other, yell, or use abusive language.
- Stay on the topic and in the present tense.
- Admit that you feel angry. Don't "let things go" to the point that you feel like exploding: Air your feelings.
- Do not interrupt.
- Take responsibility for your own feelings by using "I" statements ("I feel _____" instead of "You make me feel _____").
- Work to solve, not to blame. You really are a team, and it's okay to have different points of view.
- Don't speak for him: Avoid saying "You do _____" and "You feel _____." Let him tell you.
- If you must take a break, be sure to say that you'll be back. Never walk out in a huff! And if it's late, declare a temporary truce, go to bed, and reschedule.

Deal Breakers and Ultimatums

There is a lesson to be learned from each and every argument you have. For example, you may win the battle using your customary tactics, but you could lose the war. In the long run, ultimatums don't work and you can wind up with a truce built on long-standing resentments. When you are facing what you feel is a deal breaker in your relationship, there are several important things to do:

1. **Delivery service:** Deliver your message carefully, not impulsively or in a rage. Try something like: "I'm not giving you an ultimatum. It is your prerogative to do what you want to do, but this is what I need. If our agendas don't match up, they don't, but don't expect me to carry on this way if it's wrong for me." This is a mature way to approach the subject in which you acknowledge his preference but also make it clear that you value your own. In the end, if he doesn't want what you want or can't do what you're asking, it won't happen, even if you stomp around and throw a tantrum. But if he's on the fence or wrestling with issues, a mature calm approach is much more effective when it comes to getting your message across and earning you respect.

2. **Be on time:** Timing matters as much as choice of words and tone of voice. It is not the time to talk when you are upset, when he is tired, or when you both are distracted by other pressures. Try scheduling time to talk. If he refuses or evades you, you may have to accept that you don't have a problem-solving partner and it is time to seriously consider if you can stay in the relationship.

3. **Don't be a sore loser:** You must be mentally and emotionally prepared to lose the battle. That does not mean that you must feel happy about it, but you can't have it all.

Sex and the Internet

For your last boyfriend, surfing the Web was probably as close to second nature as showering. Your older man, on the other hand, is probably not nearly as intimate with a PC (or a Mac), depending on his age. His assistant, or maybe even his teenage son, checks his e-mail, and he types with two fingers. Unless, of course, he's in the biz or his business is heavily reliant on computer knowledge. But in that case, you're the one who's out of the computer loop. Regardless of his Internet savvy, at least you can heave a sigh of relief about the fact that he doesn't have a Myspace page. Whew!

One thing your twenty-five- and fifty-five-year-old beaus do have common, however, is the fact that a significantly larger portion of their brain is dedicated to sex than ours. While a woman's interest in sex changes depending on the month and the phase of life, men don't have cramps, birthing, or menopause to think about—which, in part, leads them to think about sex more often, and more consistently than women do. Add that biological wiring to procreate as much and as often as possible to the basic compulsive personality pitfalls, and you may have a ready and ripe consumer of . . . online sex. Despite the births and deaths of thousands of start-ups since the beginning of the Internet, Internet sex—from dating to chat rooms, porn, and fetish communities—has consistently grown and shown revenue year to year.

In Her Words

"When Larry got caught surfing porn at his job, I was mortified. He was put on probation and had to go to therapy through his job. At first we were encouraged not to have any computers at home, then it was recommended we have a 'nanny' program to monitor him. I felt cheated on, like I didn't know the man I had married."

Enid, 35

The good news is that anonymity and community has allowed sexual health information to be easily accessed, and relationships—however long or short—to happen regardless of the constraints of distance. Moreover, a study in the *Journal of Applied Psychology* reported that Internet porn did not increase sexual violence. The bad news, not withstanding, is that Internet addiction, especially related to sex, has become a real problem for thousands of couples who find themselves stunned by the havoc this can wreak on intimacy and trust.

In Her Words

"I'd go to sleep and Steve would stay up to 'catch up on e-mails.' Finally once he stepped away from the computer, and I got up to find him chatting with someone. I was furious! They spoke to each other like old lovers. When confronted, he told me they had exchanged pictures but never met in real life."

Carol, 39

What's a Girl to Do?

If you find yourself angry and frustrated when your guy is in front of the computer for long spells, ask yourself:

- Does your man have traits of obsessive compulsive or obsessive compulsive personality disorder?
- What are his preoccupations? (Money, cleanliness, perfection all around, sex?)
- Does he have the old "addictive personality"?
- Have there been noticeable changes in your sex life (much more or less)?

If your answers point you in the direction of that hunch, check it out. While we're not advocating invading his privacy by breaking into his e-mail, you may really need to confront him.

Cheating—Virtually or Otherwise

The definition of cheating has always been complicated. No, it's not just about "the man" in the relationship getting caught with his pants down after hours with his secretary, or hubby coming home to find the gardener and his wife in bed under the sheets. The jargon, euphemisms, and technicalities around what is considered sex in today's computer-oriented world are way beyond the birds and bees of yesterday. Defining what cheating is for you is personal and complex but always has an emotional component. It's not necessarily just about sex with someone else—it's about intimacy. So be it real or virtual sex, your personal definition of what crosses the line may be radically different than the next gal's, or even than—gasp—your significant other's, especially when generational perspectives start to clash. If he didn't live out his dating years with dozens of opportunities to "chat" online, this kind of cyber connection could be more innocuous to you and really upsetting to him. Then again, more opportunities to "hook up" don't automatically turn a "good man" into a raving Internet sex fiend! It just means that when the going gets tough, there is a much more convenient way to find a connection—be it emotional or sexual.

Of course, there are hypocrisy and double standards all over the place regardless of age differences. For example, you "know" your flirting isn't going anywhere, but if he did that—watch out! Or he "just kissed her once," but you'd better not even smile back at another guy.

At the end of the day, remember what we told you earlier: Communicate about what's happening between the two of you with honesty and resolve. Don't freak out and scream your head off because he'll probably just shut down. If you notice unusual changes in your sex life or your daily and weekly routine together, and things are going poorly, don't be afraid to ask him. Make sure that you, too, are open to talking about issues involving sex, and, if necessary, consult a professional.

> ♫ The number one reason for cheating that men list is boredom or that they crave "variety." Women, on the other hand, say they need attention. Men's cheating tends to be centered around intercourse, whereas women cite emotional connections (and possibly sex as well).

Yes, a man's brain has a significantly larger portion dedicated to sex, whereas our hormones send us on a monthly trip from lust to connection to family/childrearing, home, and personal needs. The lack of these hormonal fluctuations in a man's body keeps him in that lusty chase-and-conquer phase well into adulthood (though his testosterone peaks at nineteen). Being monogamous is an intellectual choice and should not define the success of a couple. Being monogamous but miserable doesn't mean you've done a better job than your swinging, happy neighbors.

Defining Cheating in Your Relationship

Because men and women are so different in their definition, there is often a stalemate where one blames the other for the tepid sex. Fears of the other's cheating may be real or imagined—and this adds to the stress at the time. Talk to your partner about their definition of cheating. It might not be comfortable, but talk about each one of these questions to make sure you are on the same page. For example:

- Is watching porn, either online or on DVD, cheating? If not, how does it make the nonviewer feel? What does it fulfill for the viewer?
- Is chatting in a provocative and flirtatious way online cheating? Is it threatening? Why or why not? What would happen if the shoe were on the other foot?
- What about friends of the opposite sex at work? What is okay?
- Is "phone sex" with someone else really cheating? Does it feel like cheating? Does it feel like it can lead to something else? Talk about how it makes each of you feel.
- Is oral sex taken as seriously as intercourse?

🎀 Tom W. Smith, author of the *National Opinion Research Center's Reports on Sexual Behavior* (April 2003), notes that, "In the last twelve to fifteen years, the 'infidelity gap' has narrowed, as the percent of previously or currently married women ever involved in an affair has risen while the percent of previously or currently married men ever involved in an affair has remained stable."

Are You a Love Addict?

Sam came into therapy because he was the older man, had just started dating a woman, and wanted more than anything for the new relationship to last. Problem was, his track record was bad, in fact, miserable. Once the lust gave out, he bailed, and was on to the next relationship. While this pattern was all right in college, and even afterward, it fed into his definition of himself of a wild bachelor. Now he knew intellectually that Isabel was a fantastic woman, he wanted a family, and he certainly wasn't getting any younger. The commitment scared him, and, more than anything else, the rush of a new relationship was addictive—whether it was cheating on his current girlfriend or just getting another.

If we can put libido or commitment issues aside (which is unrealistic, but let's do so for argument's sake), new love is like a drug. We've pointed out earlier how it centers in the same part of the brain that amphetamine addiction does. You know the feeling: You feel high, like you're on cloud nine, and can't stop thinking about him. For him, the feeling is the same. What if you never make it to the next phase where the lusty, drugged-up phase moves to affection, when you come off cloud nine, regain your appetite, and are able to argue, discuss, and even disagree?

There is such a thing as a sex or love addict. After lovely phase one, the addict starts feeling bored and looking for the next relationship that will offer that craved neurochemical intensity. Often, this addiction is wound up with psychological factors such as needing to feel in love in order to feel adequate as a person or remotely attractive. It can also be symptomatic of poor communication skills in a relationship that might otherwise be viable if there were better communication and more intimacy.

> Cheating had torn apart Jason's first marriage. Then he had dated almost compulsively for years. Melissa hoped she was different, that somehow she could get him to settle down. Jason talked to her about not feeling like he could stay interested after the initial rush wore off. While he baulked at therapy, he didn't want to lose her so he started exploring how his unrealistic expectations for relationships led him to disappointment and how the move to affection felt like a permanent loss of lust.

When Lust Wears Off

It's impossible to stand at a grocery store line and not see a magazine cover line that beckons you with provocative promises: "10 Sure-Fire Ways to Put the Lust Back in your Marriage," "Reignite the Passion in Your Relationship," or "How to Make that Not-so-Hot Sex Sizzle Again."

You might roll your eyes, look over your shoulder, then flip to that very page, hoping you'll find out that secret before it's your turn to check out, because, after all, the lusty, passionate feelings do seem to wane, more or less quickly, in every relationship.

In addition to whatever that "trick" is, a lot of women we interviewed also wanted to feel less pressure all around to have hot, crazy, passionate sex at 10 P.M. when all they wanted to do was turn in and drift off to CNN after a grueling day at the office in three-inch heels.

How, then, will this relationship with your OM be different? Well, perhaps, on the basis of years of experience, he either knows those coveted tricks, too, or perhaps he just understands women a bit better and realizes that some good listening and a foot massage during the week can indeed translate into hot sex during the weekend. Or better yet: His testosterone levels are lower and he no longer needs sex morning, noon, and night!

The change from desperate, passionate, rip-your-clothes-off, can't-stop-thinking-about-him dates to the calmer affection and daily living is not your fault or his, it's simply a matter of a biochemical move from lust to affection and attachment. And that is a good thing! Otherwise, you'd never get any work done. That being said, although the next phase of love is comfortable and wired to lead to long-term attachment, all couples miss that all-consuming passion they had "in the beginning." Forget about the gimmicks. The reality is that you can't biologically turn your brain back to that first phase; but you can keep lusty moments in your relationship while enjoying the relaxing affection and different attachment-type love of the next phase. Here's what to avoid:

- Stress and sleep deprivation—they will kill sex drive.
- Too much sex—anticipation is a great aphrodisiac.
- Brief or no foreplay—and not just the physical foreplay, but the mental foreplay women need.

In addition to all these factors, we all live in a world where everything is fast, loud, glossy, and streamlined. So while the ability to multitask and do things becomes faster and more efficient, sex and love still need the slow titillating dance they always did. They need planning and work, and people have gotten so used to solutions that come with a push of a button or phone call that it takes mental energy to slow down and remember that love and sex are ever-changing processes that need attention and care.

It is important to keep all the aforementioned in mind because the statistical trends that show women waiting longer to get married and divorce rates not slowing down raise questions about whether monogamy is natural, if it is possible to be happy in a marriage forever, or if men are necessary at all.

QUOTES FROM THE COUCH:
RECOGNIZE YOURSELF IN ANY OF THESE?

"I thought that the excitement of Josh being different, older, would make the excitement of the relationship last longer than my past relationships. When things started losing that spark and feeling routine, I was really disappointed. I wanted to go back to that first month when I felt jittery and crazy in love."—Arlene, 41

"John was more traditional; it wasn't immediately a sleep-over party like with guys my age. The dating, the waiting, and the introducing him to my friends and family slowly gave the whole process a different flavor. He was busy and had a lot of responsibilities and he didn't like cutting corners to just see me hurriedly. I felt like he knew (whether it was from doing it right or wrong before) how that beginning spark was important."—Jessica, 24

"We went from magical first kiss, to lust, to comfortable and cuddly, to bored in a matter of weeks. I admit it, I was pissed. Andy rushed through the beginning of our relationship and got way too comfortable way too quickly. I felt myself getting antsy and bored with the routine faster than ever before. I'm worried."—Chloe, 38

"I felt pressured to keep the sex really lively so that Frank wouldn't think about cheating on me. To me, sex getting into more of a routine meant failure. I'd gotten blamed for my boyfriends' straying in the past and I didn't want it to happen in this relationship, too. I kept thinking that he'd chosen to be with me in part because I was supposed to be younger and livelier. All that pressure made me focus on myself less, which meant I rarely had fun."
—Karen, 33

"Part of the reason Jim had left his last wife was because of his being bored in the bedroom. I made sure he understood he had half the responsibility for keeping things interesting. Besides, having sex with the same person has some great upsides as far as being comfortable and not feeling like you have to perform."—Alexandra, 35

"I've always ended up straying or moving on to the next relationship when the magic wears off. I'm just addicted to that newness. It doesn't mean I don't love my guy, but I hate the routine."—Jennifer, 29

A Parting Word: Sex and Self-Esteem

Getting the "lust" back means different things for men and women. Men will talk about sex that was spontaneous; women, initiating and variety. Women will miss the foreplay, the attention to her verbal and nonverbal requests, and intense focus on her and her sensuality. One of the most talked about topics in couples and group therapy is one that is hard for men to grasp: Women need to feel sexy to have good sex. Self-esteem is crucial for fostering desire. The mind, specifically the limbic system (which has been described as the emotional seat of the brain), is the single most important organ when it comes to sexual arousal and desire, which means that desire actually begins long before any body parts touch. Never forget that desire begins with a state of mind.

Glossary

This glossary is designed for use with this book. Please note that the terms are defined by how they relate to younger-woman/older-man relationships.

Absent father:
Type of fathering women may unconsciously internalize, a "daddy style." With or without the promise of being there, Dad was not. Feeling ignored, unloved, and not good enough to capture Dad's attention, a little girl is on a seesaw and grows into a woman who bounces between her mistrust or hatred of men and an intense quest to capture their love and affection.

Accommodation syndrome:
When a woman first falls in love with an older man, she may want to take care of him as if he were both a lover and a child. But if he becomes accustomed to the abundance of care, the woman gets stuck in that supercharged accommodating version of herself.

Adult kid:
When a child is under the false impression that he or she is the adult, and speaks to the new wife using adult terms and with a very adult tone of voice.

Angry man:

A man whose irritability starts showing through once he's comfortable with a relationship. He constantly displaces his anger onto inappropriate targets and personalizes the behavior of others even when it's clear they have nothing to do with him.

Angry father:

Type of fathering women may unconsciously internalize, a "daddy style." Whatever his other personality traits, Dad's temper raged from zero to ninety in sixty seconds, and the little girl either walked on eggshells in an attempt to be invisible or rose up like a phoenix from the ashes to battle him back. The child may grow into a woman who harbors both tendencies within her psyche. While this dynamic can be recreated in any age scenario, in the case of the younger woman, she may be taking on a guy close to Daddy's age in order to prove to herself that she can overcome him.

Anxiety disorders:

The most common mental health problems are classified in a group under "anxiety disorders," which include panic disorders, phobias, generalized anxiety disorder, obsessive-compulsive disorder (OCD), or post-traumatic stress disorder (PTSD).

Assertive behavior:

Calmly, clearly, and firmly delineating boundaries and limits. Being assertive is when you can express yourself in a calm, objective manner in a situation where emotion could easily get the upper hand.

Attachment phase:

This phase in a relationship is characterized by very mellow feelings and the drive to "nest," and may have a lot to do with hormones. With orgasm, oxytocin and vasopressin, the hormones that are an integral part of breastfeeding, spike. Both of these hormones are associated with feelings of deep attachment, so a woman may feel intense union with a man after a sex-intense union that, in reality, has not yet been established via more everyday routes or experiences. Moreover, with an orgasm, there is a surge in dopamine, and the feelings created by this excess can even trick a woman into believing that she's falling for a guy she has only had casual sex with.

Attraction phase:
In a relationship, this stage is driven by neurotransmitters called monoamines, which are structurally similar to the amphetamines that stimulate the production of adrenaline in the body. (Adrenaline is responsible for that heart-racing good feeling that comes over a person when attracted to another.)

Awe factor:
Maureen Dowd (author of *Are Men Necessary?*) theorizes that successful men don't want fascinating women; they just want women who are awed by them.

Bowen, Murray:
Originator of the Systems Family Therapy.

Bray, James:
Author of *Stepfamilies* (Broadway Books, 1999). Bray states that early on in the relationship children view stepparents similar to a coach or camp counselor.

Bulldozing:
When the kiddies defiantly push right on over a poorly set limit.

Button pushers:
Whether it's a pet peeve or a controversial topic, these kids head straight for it, making adults feel exasperated and tense.

Chops buster:
The friend of the OM who teases the new woman to the point of pissing her off, then eases back. Then he starts again and repeats the pattern. Later calls her a good sport.

Chronology disparity:
When a difference in age means that each person in a couple experiences age-related events years apart from the other. In other words, when spouses are close in age, life changes happen in unison, whereas for a couple in which the man is significantly older, age-related events happen at significantly different times and result in significantly different experiences.

Cocktail of hope and sex:
That initial chemistry that is powerful enough to make a woman think that she is truly in love. Often women feel drawn to a man by a combination of emotion and sexual attraction. That emotion may actually be a combination of the familiar feelings experienced in childhood toward fathers, mixed in with the sense and hope of a real resolution to the conflict she had with him, or Mom had with him, this time around. When the early sexual attraction mellows, she can be left with a connection that is fraught with many of the same problems experienced firsthand in childhood.

Control guy:
Protective and gentlemanly slowly crosses the line to controlling and all-consuming in this man. His "take-charge personality" may start out as refreshing, and being able to lean on him was a welcome change, but it can quickly become stifling.

Crenshaw, Theresa L.:
Author of *The Alchemy of Love and Lust* (Penguin Group, 1996), who points out that, "As a woman gets older she usually manifests more traditionally 'masculine' traits—decisiveness, assertiveness, physical sexuality, and independence. Men expand their 'female' dimension of touching, tenderness, insight, patience, and understanding."

Date span:
The age range that a woman will consider when dating. Statistics tell us that the older-man/younger-woman couple will continue to become more and more prevalent. Men are living longer than ever before, retiring younger, and looking and acting more youthful than ever, whereas women are waiting longer to marry, and divorces from first (and second) marriages continue to rise; as a result, more women in their late twenties, thirties, and forties are widening their "date span."

Dellasega, Cherly:
Author of *Forced to Be Family: A Guide for Living with Sinister Sisters, Drama Mamas, and Infuriating In-Laws* (John Wiley & Sons, 2007).

Dictator:
The OM as a stepfather who freely imposes his "rules" on her children without realizing that they are just starting to get used to his presence and may not be the least bit familiar with his way of doing things.

Ego boundary:
The forces that separate people and make them distinct. The "self" is pictured as a round circle, encased in a ring, which is called the "boundary." A person's sense of self and identity is maintained or preserved by appropriately flexible but strong boundaries.

Elektra complex:

A Freudian term that refers to a woman's unconscious desire to possess her father and do away with her mother. The resolution of the complex, according to Freud, happens when little girls make a solid identification with their mothers and rediscover their fathers—say in terms of their personality traits or style of relating—in a relationship with a mature man.

Fathering styles:

Types of fathering women may unconsciously internalize. They include: overprotective, overbearing, absent, supercritical, angry, yes man, loving heart, and martyr. As a result of this internalization, some women will seek out a man who treats them as their fathers did, or who even shares similar physical characteristics; on the other hand, there are women who will do exactly the opposite in an effort to avoid past pain.

Father-spouse:

Daughters who report very positive relationships with their fathers tend to choose boyfriends or husbands with similar facial characteristics. Some research reports that women are actually attracted to men who smell like Dad!

Fear-of-friend rejection:

Occurs when her friends are being as rambunctious as usual but she finds herself tensing up, hoping they won't be too juvenile in front of her older man. She braces herself for their reactions in private the next day.

Frenemy:

The kind of friend who often plays the game of "one-up-man-ship," which is the equivalent of outdoing friends in any act or even conversation.

Furman, Beliza Ann:
Author of the book *Younger Women-Older Men* (Barricade Books, 1999).

Growth hormone:
The hormone that helps fuel growth during childhood and maintains tissues and organs throughout life. Beginning at around age forty, the pituitary gland—the pea-sized structure at the base of your brain where growth hormone is made—slowly reduces the amount of the hormone it produces. Reduced growth hormone results in loss of strength and energy, increased body fat (especially around the abdomen), and psychological changes. In sum, the realities of old age.

Half-your-age-plus-seven rule:
A mathematical formula that purports to judge whether the age difference in an intimate relationship is socially acceptable. The age difference that is generally accepted by modern society varies directly with the age of the individuals involved in the relationship; that is, larger differences are more acceptable with older individuals.

Heart of gold guy:
Dorky; he's fodder for *The 40-Year-Old Virgin* but his sweetness is irresistible, and the confidence that comes with his age and mastery of profession doesn't hurt. Maybe he brings out the mother in a woman. This guy lights up when she appears, wags his tail, and takes every opportunity to make her happy . . . then trips on his own shoelaces.

Home wrecker:
(also called "gold digger" or the "object of a midlife crisis") The younger girlfriend or younger second wife who is accused of going after a man's professional knowledge and contacts, his insurance, money,

and credit, and of creating strife between him and his adult
children.

Infidelity gap:
The percentage of previously or currently married women ever
involved in an affair has risen while the percentage of previously
or currently married men ever involved in an affair has remained
stable.

Insecure guy:
Mixed with humor, insecurity in a man can come off as self-
deprecation and can even be funny, but the insecure guy needs the
awe factor and constant ego stroking to feel good enough about
himself to be pleasant company. It's possible that his "sensitivity"
will become paranoia and his "dependability" smothering.

Insecure wife:
The woman who constantly worries out loud about her looks and
asks several times how old she appears to be. Is continually looking for her husband, and talking about how many things they did
together and how perfect they are for each other.

Instant love:
The myth that love between family members will happen
immediately.

Kitchen wars:
These are emotional battles among female relatives that are larger
in magnitude and impact than the offenses of even dearest friends.
More love, more difficulty, more anguish, and more of everything are the hallmarks of both distant and close female relationships within families.

Lightning rods:
Children who inject themselves in the middle, taking the heat from the two parents in an argument. The way to protect these kids is to define roles and give reassurance.

Limbic system:
The emotional seat of the brain. It is the single most important component when it comes to sexual arousal and desire, which means that desire may begin long before any body parts touch.

Love addict:
The person who, after the first phase of a relationship has been established, starts feeling bored and begins searching for the next relationship that will offer that craved neurochemical intensity.

Love sponges:
Children who are constantly seeking attention and affection (the operative word here being "constantly"). Whatever the underlying cause, this behavior has been reinforced by their receiving all the attention they crave.

Love-is-blind phenomenon:
The neurochemical effects that render a woman incapable of seeing a guy clearly. Unfortunately, when the romantic fog clears, she may already be walking down the aisle.

Loving heart:
Type of fathering women may unconsciously internalize, a "fathering style." Dad was not perfect, but the daughter always knew that this man loved her unconditionally. This is the kind of love that cultivates self-love. Becoming accustomed to feeling important and deeply cared for can create in a woman the ability to "have your own back" in relationships.

Male menopause:

Between the ages of forty and fifty-five, men may experience a phenomenon known as andropause, which is characterized by a drop in testosterone. The bodily changes occur very gradually in men and may be accompanied by changes in attitudes and moods, fatigue, a loss of energy, sex drive, and physical agility.

Martyr:

Type of fathering women may unconsciously internalize, a "daddy style." Dad was always there for his children and, boy, did he let them know it. In this scenario, the daughter is made to feel heavy amounts of guilt for the smallest slight in any interpersonal situation. As an adult, for her the older man is quite possibly the man to be taken care of, and alternately to be left behind as she runs off with her peers as an escape.

May-December romance:

A relationship in which there is a significant age discrepancy.

Missing out:

The worry about "falling out of the loop." Consequently, a hesitation to get married may be characterized by such thoughts as: "I feel like if I get married, it will make me lose focus on my work," or "I won't spend time with my friends like before." Some women are frightened of giving up a chapter in their lives, and consider putting marriage off.

Modern younger woman:

In her thirties or forties, she has come of age in an era when women are waiting longer to get married because they are enjoying their careers and independence. This phenomenon of staggered chronology has systematically destroyed the notion of the wide-eyed younger woman in her stereotypically more submissive role.

Molloy, John T.:
Author of *Why Men Marry Some Women and Not Others* (Warner Books, 2004)

Multigenerational transmission process:
The manner in which, according to Murray Bowen's Systems Family Therapy, family members relate to each other emotionally. It is transmitted in the family from generation to generation (say father-wife or father-daughter). As new spouses marry into the family and play their roles, they repeat and maintain these patterns of emotional relationships.

Negotiating, youngster style:
An art children are capable of perfecting in order to wear a parent down.

Object-relation model:
Refers to the theory that people unconsciously pick mates who remind them of internalized versions of their parents, and relate to them with the same emotional patterns. "Imago" therapy is also a popular couples' format that postulates that the "imago" is a mental image of all the combined traits of the primary caretakers that reside deep within the subconscious.

Open-minded friend:
One of "his" friends who is happy to meet you, the new woman. He or she treats you as if you already have something in common—which you do! They ask questions about you, your job, your family.

Optimal response:
An opinion that is diplomatically stated in such a way that it neither offends nor humiliates. It is not evasive or angry; in fact, it adds to the relationship.

Overbearing:
Type of fathering women may unconsciously internalize, a "daddy style." Dad was overinvolved in his daughter's everyday life and an intruder in her emotional life. This is a style that can lead to shutdown, withdrawal, or disconnection from personal and intimate feelings and desires. Often this leads to the creation of the "selfless" woman, the martyr, who forfeits all of her desires and needs to satisfy others.

Overprotective:
Type of fathering women may unconsciously internalize, a "daddy style." Dad monitored everything you ate, wore, and watched, and everyone you socialized with like a hawk. Nothing and nobody was good enough for his daughter, which can instill fear and anxiety about taking reasonable and necessary risks in life. This is also a style that can breed the culture of victimhood: No matter who wronged this woman or why, someone else is at fault; she is the innocent bystander in a world full of thugs.

Overpunish:
Going beyond the normal limits of discipline; for example, taking toys or privileges away for a week. For little ones, they should be withheld for five to ten minutes per year of age.

Phantom first wife:
The first wife who is always hovering around in pictures, or in conversational references.

Phantom stepfather:
The OM as a stepfather who manages to dart around and in between the children. Gently but deftly puts off their requests for attention.

Projected anxiety:
The amount of time a woman spends worrying about how long she'll be all right before the older man is too old for her.

Propagating state of mind:
Being with a younger woman can actually propel an older guy into wanting more children—even if when she met him he felt as if he had enough offspring from a prior marriage. Feeling as if he "still has it" goes a long way when looking for a new lease on life.

Prostate:
The walnut-sized gland that makes and stores semen in men. Located just below the bottom of the bladder and in front of the rectum, it becomes enlarged as a man ages, and creates some very incommodious urinary problems. More than half of sixty-year-old men and as many as 90 percent of men in their seventies and eighties have some symptoms of benign prostatic hyperplasia (BPH).

Protector:
The guy who wants to be assured that his friend, her older man, will be taken care of. Asks a lot of background questions. The new woman will have to try her hardest not to ask, "Did I get the job?" but relaxes significantly once she's jumped through a few hoops.

Real age or "body age":
The idea that your chronological age is really just a number.

Redistributing power:
Disparity in age may actually redistribute power with more equality. More important, from a relationship standpoint, couples have to be psychologically equal partners who must collaborate to survive—and this is what many women crave.

Repetition compulsion:

A phenomenon from psychoanalytic theory in which people are driven to re-enact emotional experiences from early childhood without awareness or intent, over and over again. Thus a woman may find herself inexplicably drawn to men who have a constellation of personality traits similar to either her mother's or her father's. Time after time she will find herself in emotional interactions with her boyfriends that mirror what she witnessed between her parents.

Revised older-man/younger-woman duo:

A scenario in which, given rejuvenation and the push for eternal youth and extension of life, the "younger" woman may be thirty-five or forty, and the older man, ten to twenty years older.

Right guy, wrong reason:

A situation in which a woman is attracted to a man, drawn by personality traits that are similar to those of a parent or childhood caretaker. There are several different principles from classical psychological theory that illustrate this very phenomenon. To the extent that this is true, interacting with familiar personality traits in men recreates for some women familiar interpersonal patterns and emotions from childhood in current relationships, and drives the way people experience and relate to each other.

Second adulthood for women:

According to author Suzanne Braun Levine (*Inventing the Rest of Our Lives*, Thorndike Press, 2005) women can all look forward to two adulthoods: "If you figure that the first adulthood lasts from twenty-five to fifty, you have statistically at least that much time ahead of you until you're seventy-five."

Second-wife etiquette:
The rules and conventions of polite behavior expected from a second-wife. For more on this, check out Second Wives Café (online support for second wives and step moms), Second Wives Clubs (Sisterhood for Stepmoms), Second Wives Coalition (of the National Family Justice Association), and Steptalk.org. More guidelines and support are on the horizon.

Self:
A sense of our unique existence among others that may be considered the foundation of one's personal identity. Identity, then, is a person's subjective concept of oneself as an individual. An authentic self is not a hollow representation of whom others want or need one to be.

***Sex and the City* syndrome:**
Esther M. Berger, a Beverly Hills certified financial planner and money manager, defines this as afflicting women who, like character Carrie Bradshaw, are burdened with high debt and who have more or less invested their entire net worth in clothing and shoes.

Sexy grandma:
A younger woman, possibly in her twenties or thirties, who is married to an older man who has grandchildren, which technically makes her a grandmother (well, stepgrandmother).

Side-by-side relating:
The difference in how the sexes relate. The experts say that men relate actively (e.g., playing a sport or working on a project together), whereas women favor face-to-face analysis, or, as some men say, the "talkity, talk, talk" approach.

Skeptic:
The one who asks questions of the new younger woman that verge on the inappropriate. Almost comes out and asks if she really knows what she is "in for." Comes out with several examples of May-December couples that didn't make it.

Soon-to-be-divorced man:
A man who is pulled in two different directions and is feeling confused and/or guilty. For the woman, it is an emotional rollercoaster: One minute she is the center of attention while at other times she takes a clear backseat to his former life.

Spoiler:
The OM as a stepfather or mother's boyfriend who lets the kids get away with everything. He spoils them and then turns the other cheek when they're out of line.

Stages of love:
According to biochemists, love is comprised of three distinct states: lust, attraction, and attachment. Attachment predominates in more enduring, committed relationships. Lust is governed by a potent cocktail of hormones, including estrogen or testosterone.

Starter husband:
A woman's first husband, often the one she started a family with.

Stepcoupling:
The joining of two families to make a "blended one."

Stepfamily:
The family of the future. Today, one of every four children is a stepchild. Some predict that by the year 2020, stepfamilies will outnumber nuclear families.

Stepfather:

Like stepmother, the term stepfather has certain negative con-notations. In our society, the word "divorce" is still a dirty one fraught with all the sadness and trauma that may accompany the breakup of a marriage and family, and stepfather carries some of that baggage. Obviously not all stepfathers ride in on a white horse and save the day, but, on the other hand, there is the pos-sibility that they can offer peace where there was conflict.

Step-monster:

Mean and evil stepmothers come to mind, ones who monopo-lize father's attention and manage to negotiate an allowance cut. The fairy-tale scenario has the father widowed, and blind to this woman's mission to control the family.

Supercritical:

Type of fathering women may unconsciously internalize, a "daddy style." In this scenario, nothing was good enough for Dad. This style can lead to chronic self-criticism, low self-esteem, and futile perfectionism. It can also lead to a struggle between setting unre-alistic expectations and abandoning those expectations altogether due to low frustration tolerance.

System changer:

An outsider, often the boyfriend or girlfriend of a mother or father, who comes along and disrupts the homeostatic system of a family.

Teaser:

The OM as a stepfather who believes that he can "toughen them up" with a little adversity, namely practical jokes and teasing.

Testosterone Replacement Therapy (TRT):

As a man ages, the amount of testosterone in his body gradually declines. This natural decline starts after age thirty and continues throughout life. Adequate testosterone levels are important for maintaining muscle bulk, adequate levels of red blood cells, bone growth, sense of well-being, and sexual function.

Ventral tegmental area and the caudate nucleus:

Parts of the brain that get stimulated and charged up by the release of "lust/love" hormones and neurotransmitters. The frontal lobes, on the other hand, are the uniquely human part of the brain that help people evaluate what they're doing and make rational choices.

Victimized and divorced guy:

A man whose litany sounds something like this: "I put all my money into fixing up her place, I put her through school and I gave her backrubs . . . I tried harder, brought her flowers, listened, but she wasn't satisfied." This man is available and may be attentive, but a woman is bound to wonder when he is going to get off the pity pot.

Widow-phobia:

A hesitation to get married plagued by thoughts such as, "What if he dies within a few years of our marriage. . . . What if he dies way before I do?" Many women agonizing over these questions forget that many forty-year olds have died of sudden heart attacks, and anyone, at any age, can get hit by a bus. Same goes with concerns about nursing him in his old age.

Wild one:

A man who comes and goes as he pleases and is up-front about not being so good at making plans. "I don't like to be held to anything, I really value spontaneity" is the typical mantra. Bottom line here is that sometimes he's a breath of fresh air, other times his significant other wants to kill him—all within the same ten minutes.

Wise guy:
A man who recognizes and compliments a woman's achievements and doesn't try to change her. He listens during fights and learns new relationship information, giving the impression that he's had sisters and knows how to live with women.

Yes man:
Type of fathering women may unconsciously internalize, a "daddy style." Dad gave you everything you wanted and more. Maybe the little girl had to whine, beg, flirt, and wheedle, but she got the toys, the clothes, the vacations, the car, the college, the credit card, and so on. In this scenario, the dad unwittingly stunted his daughter's ability to endure pain, to be comfortable with delaying gratification, or to take pleasure in the rewards of her own hard work.

Additional Resources

Alchemy of Love and Lust by Theresa L. Crenshaw (Penguin Group, 1996)

Are Men Necessary? When Sexes Collide by Maureen Dowd (Penguin Group, 2006)

Brain Sex: The Real Difference Between Men and Women by Anne Moir (Delta 1992)

The Empowered Woman's Guide to Pleasuring a Man by Ian Kerner (Harper Collins, 2006)

Essential Difference: The Truth About the Male and Female Brains and the Truth About Autism by Simon Baron-Cohen (Perseus Books Group, 2003)

Family Therapy in Clinical Practice by Murray Bowen (John Aranson Inc., 1990)

Female Brain by Louann Brizendine (Morgan Road Books, 2006)

Forced to Be Family: A Guide for Living with Sinister Sisters, Drama Mamas, and Infuriating In-Laws by Cherly Dellasega (John Wiley & Sons, 2007)

Inventing the Rest of Our Lives by Suzanne Braun Levine (Thorndike Press, 2005)

Sex on the Brain by Daniel G. Amen (Hamony, 2007)

Singled Out: How Singles Are Stereotyped, Stigmatized, and Ignored, and Still Live Happily Ever After by Bella DePaulo (St. Martin's Press, 2006)

Social Intelligence: The New Science of Human Relationships by Daniel Goleman (Bantam, 2006)

SOS Help for Emotions: Managing Anxiety, Anger, and Depression by Lynn Clark (Parents Press, 2001)

Why Men Marry Some Women and Not Others by John T. Molloy (Warner Books, 2004)

Younger Women-Older Men by Beliza Ann Furman (Barricade Books, 1999)

Index

Index

jaded by, 167–69, 170
reasons for, 5
victimized guy and, 22–23
Domineering types, 24–25

Elektra complex, 128
Emotional turmoil, 34–36
Ex-wives, 4, 44–45, 78

Family
blended, 91–92
culture clashes and, 79–81
introductions to, 71
meeting his, 77–79
parent reactions, 69–73
value systems, 81–82
Father figure, older man as, 130–33,
141–43
Fathering styles, 134–39
Father issues, 71, 72, 128–29, 133–41
Female expectations, 187–89
Fertility issues, 153
Fighting, 189–93
Financial stability, 15–16, 175–76
Freudian theories, 128
Friends
confronting your, 57–58
as enemies, 56–57
inappropriate behavior by, 51–52
interaction between boyfriend and,
52–53
introductions to, 48–51
meeting his, 63–67
reactions of, 47–48, 53–57,
59–67

Gender roles, 177–78
Girls, 96
Girls' night out, 41–43
Growth hormone, 158–59

Hair issues, 154–57
"Half-your-age-plus-seven" rule, 16–17
Health-related issues, 145–63
Heart-of-Gold Guy, 24
Hefner, Hugh, 10
HIV/AIDS, 150–51
Hollywood, 17
"How do I look?" questions, 38–40

Identity
loss of, 121–23
maintaining, 111, 112
pursuing your, 123–25
Illness, 43–44
Imago therapy, 129
Individual time, 41–42
Indulgent fathers, 136–37
Infidelity, 14, 196–98
Insecure Guy, 23–24
Internet dating, viii
Internet sex, 193–96

Life changes, 12–14
Life expectancy, viii
Life pursuits, 123–25
Love addiction, 198–99

Male menopause, 157–59
Marriage, readiness for, 165–78
Martyrs, 138
Math Game, 17
Maturity, 5
May-December romances, 14–15
Mental health, 160
Midlife crisis, vii, 8–9
Money issues, 15–16, 175–76
Mothers, reactions of, 84–85
Multigenerational transmission
process, 129

Object relations, 129
Oedipus conflict, 128
Older-man/younger-woman
relationships, social acceptance of,
10–11. *See also* Relationships
Older men
acceptability of dating, 2–4
challenges of dating, 4–6
as father figure, 130–33,
141–43
reasons for attraction to younger
women by, 6–9
remarriage and, 165–78
as stepdads, 74–77
stereotypes about, 9–12, 17
traits of, 19–46
Overbearing fathers, 134
Overprotective fathers, 134

About the Authors

Belisa Vranich, Psy.D. (New York, NY), is the Dear Doctor columnist for the *New York Daily News*. She is a contributor to *Women's Health* magazine and writes a column for the *Huffington Post*. The telegenic psychologist is a regular guest on *Good Morning America*, CNN, VH1, and *Inside Edition*. She has been quoted and/or profiled in publications such as *Cosmopolitan, Spin Magazine, Seventeen*, and the *Wall Street Journal*. Belisa is also an author and public speaker in the area of health and mental health and was the Director of Public Education at the Mental Health Association of NYC. She is also the author of *The Seven Beliefs: A Step by Step Guide to Help Latinas Recognize and Overcome Depression*. She has been widely published in outlets such as *Jane* magazine, *Latina Magazine*, America Online and the *New York Post*. Dr. Belisa is single and her Web site is *www.drbelisa.com*.

Dr. Laura Grashow is a clinical psychologist who has a thriving practice in South Florida where she is well known for her highly dynamic and direct, yet compassionate, style, and her time-effective approach. She works with children, parents, and families on topics ranging from relationship issues and parenting to anxiety, depression, crises intervention, and learning problems. Dr. Grashow has been quoted in local and national media outlets such as *South Florida Parenting, New York Newsday, Men's Fitness,* and Fox Radio. Prior to establishing her practice in South Florida, she also practiced in New York City and Singapore, where she resided for two years.

Dr. Grashow is best known for her effective intervention skills and ability to foster growth in children and parents and to restore balance in dysfunctional families. In addition to her clinical expertise, she has over twelve years of experience doing clinical presentations to professional local and national associations, as well as parent and teacher workshops.

Dr. Grashow earned her doctoral degree from Yeshiva University and completed her residency in the pediatric department of the Albert Einstein College of Medicine where she spearheaded a program designed to screen young foster children for developmental disabilities or delays. She completed her internship in Newark, New Jersey at the University of Medicine and Dentistry and also trained at Bellevue Hospital in New York.

Prior to her pursuit of a career in psychology, Dr. Grashow was a classroom teacher for the New York City Public School System. Her background also includes teaching Early Childhood and Junior High School at private school settings in both New York and Florida. She is a member of the American Psychological Association and Psychology and the Arts. To learn more about Dr. Grashow, check out *www.drgrashow .com* where you can also read about how to handle some of life's toughest situations.